COSMIC SOUL

Akashic Records

Journey of a Mystic

TEZA ZIALCITA

Disclaimer:

This is not a medical intervention; it is an attunement to increase your sense of well-being. If you are receiving medical attention from a Medical Doctor, please do not discontinue what you are receiving. I am not in any sense liable for your choices. Thank you so much for your interest in this method of healing.

This book is lovingly dedicated

to my eternal son Theo.

Thank you so much for loving me,

I feel your presence every day!

I love you so much.

xoxo

Ma

Acknowledgements

Thank you for all the souls that gave their trust, and chose me as their spiritual guide. I am so honored to be a channel of divine grace.

Thank you for my beautiful children who are treasures in my life: Matt Zialcita, Tiffany Hill, Tristan Hill, and for Theo Hill, my beloved son who transitioned too soon. You broke open my heart and made me love the whole of humanity.

Thank you Alma Bella Maglaya, my compassionate, energized, loving and sassy editor for giving all you've got! You are a God sent to my path.

Thank you to my beautiful, loving designer and soul sister Linda Stelluti. You are the galactic star that shines this brightest Light in our universe.

Thank you to all of my students, friends and family that supported and loved me all through these years.

This work would not be here without the calling that the Gatekeepers and the Lords of the Akashic Records bestowed upon my life. It is a magical life that I live, with a knowing that I am fully loved by the stars in the universe. Thank you Divine Creator and Source of all that is.

Table of Contents

Editor's Note

A Divine Invitation

You have been invited to meet The Friend,

No one can resist a Divine Invitation,

That narrows down all our choices to just two:

We can come to God

Dressed for Dancing

Or

Carried on a stretcher

To God's Ward.

By Hafiz

Hello Friend, Fellow Traveller!

In Cosmic Soul, Teza Zialcita extends a divine invitation to meet The Friend. She carefully, meticulously lays out all the necessary preparations for a date with the most resplendent and sacred within. One cannot approach the shining palace weighted and dragging one's old, smelly, stuffy, outdated, ill-fitting clothes.

She provides the extensive possibilities of wardrobe change. She shows us how to wash away the useless and to trim the unnecessary. She holds your hand each step along the way to the River of Your True Essence so you can be anointed with The Life You Richly Deserve. She calls on experienced professionals, ascended masters for guidance. She helps you step into brand new shoes, so that you are ready and dressed for dancing with the Divine!

If you picked up her book, you are blessed! If it was gifted to you, doubly blessed! It has been a tremendous honor and delight to edit Cosmic Soul. It is a much needed travel guide to a realm of self-contentment exclusively available only to those who commit to paying for the ticket to get to there. The irony is that everyone has a book of their Akashic Records but most people go through life never hearing of such a treasure or having any interest to delve into its secrets.

In this book, Teza demonstrates how simple and easy it is to spread open one's wingspan, to course correct and reach the shining ballroom.

Perhaps, at first with curiosity, perhaps with trepidation, we can venture to declare our interest, pose our questions and allow our Self the silence and stillness to listen to the answers relayed back. Thus begins the pas de deux.

This book is guaranteed to enrich your life. The ripples of its power will also touch the lives of those around you. Perhaps it will benefit even the lives of those in your ancestry that gave you life. The consequences of taking the steps forward as given in this book are without limit, precisely because it reveals the nature of who we truly are; timeless, ageless, perfect, whole, complete, eternal, immortal, undying and without limit.

It was absolutely by divine design that I met Teza. I can proudly declare and I do shout it out that she is one of the best human beings I have come across thus far. She is a role model of kindness and generosity. It is never about Teza; it is about you, how she helps you shine and be the best you can be.

My friend, now you have the essence of her teachings within these pages, you are dressed for dancing! May you enjoy every step!

Alma Bella Maglaya

Acupuncture Physician, Avid Dancer

Editor

Foreword

As a teacher and healer of Akashic Records, I was in awe of the various cases of healing that I received. I wanted to share these experiences to enhance our knowledge and wisdom about our Akashic Records as a part of our collective consciousness.

To help us in our ascension process, it is important as students of the Akashic Records to be diligent when seeking knowledge. We wish to share this wisdom to humanity so we can be empowered and enlightened in our incarnation here on Mother Earth.

We are all one.

Take the courage to move forward with our lives. We can become the light to remind others of their light. Together we remember our true essence, integrating our Higher Self to guide us in our daily lives.

To simplify our lives, we need to let go of our old ways and recreate new paradigms that shift our ways of thinking. We must surrender our attachments, and face the unknown. By being fearless, we will find the courage to move forward, venturing beyond our comfort zone. This life is transient; we have to live in the present moment of our existence. We have to keep our mind and heart open to align us with our truth. Then, we can truly say that we are liberated from all attachments. Like an eagle that soars up high in the sky, overlooking the paramount view of our lifetime.

As messengers of love and light, we allow our presence to heal those who had come in touch with us. We have chosen this path because we have these blueprints as light workers.

Serve with all your heart and soul. Give without any hesitation. Receive the blessings that you deserve. In your soul's path, attune to your intuition. Develop clarity in your discernment.

The inner voice of the spirit is within you. Listen and pay attention, the messages are given for you to share. They are not yours to keep. Be aware and awake at all times.

Believe that the messages you are receiving are coming from the Source of all that is. Your Higher Self will connect to you and be your inner voice. Faith will take you into a quantum leap. Trust in the Source of all that is. Release judgment, become open and allow others to grow. We are here to support each other in our ascension process.

These messages are coming from channelings that I received from my spiritual guides and also from my experiences as a soul healer and teacher. Some of them are direct channelings from the Masters of Light. I had a close encounter with Paramahansa Yogananda in Los Angeles on the top of Mount Washington in his Self-Realization retreat center last September 2016. It was profound, surreal and unforgettable.

One of my favorite Bodhisatva is Garchen Rinpoche, who has touched my existence in this lifetime. His presence is out of this world. When I am around him, my cells dispersed into the universe. I am no longer in my body, rather I am being activated by this amazing saint. I am deeply grateful for his teachings and healings that he does for all sentient beings.

I never realized that the day would come that I could be a channel of grace. I believe we are chosen to serve and continue the work of these Masters of Light. Our souls are holographic matrices and these Masters that had lived here are eternal souls. Continually guiding us to serve and help enlighten our soul's path.

I totally surrender my life to the works of the Masters of Light. I know I am divinely guided to do this. When these written words reverberate in your ears, you will feel the divine grace. Their words have vibrations of comfort, love, light, and inner peace. They are here whispering to you softly, we are too busy with the mundane and our attachments to this world. We forget that our existence here is beyond this world. We are here to continue to pass on the torch of Light.

We are the Light bearers. Within us is a golden Light that comes from the living Source of Light. With this knowing, we are able to live a sacred life, full of happiness and bliss. We are always guarded, protected, and guided. Our task is to ask to be of service and then, totally surrender. Within this lighted path, our inner longing to be with the Source is heard. We become attuned to the high vibrations of this divine Light and love. It is imperative to be aware at all times, surrendering the things that you cannot change to God.

You are beyond the stars, you are the universe.

You are the Cosmic Soul!

Personal History

When our Akashic Records are open, we are tapping into multiple dimensions. It can be a great, ecstatic experience or it can be an awkward, uncomfortable experience. When I studied the Records in 2008, I had a surreal vision of myself in the angelic realm. It was brought to my attention that I was in Genesis. There was this huge tree of life in a paradise setting with my two year old self. I was pronounced clinically dead of Diphtheria when I was two, and I was always inquisitive and asked God "Where did I go?"

This vision confirmed to me that I met the Source of all that is, during that glimpse of heaven. There were four Archangels that I met: Raphael, Michael, Gabriel and Uriel. They were preparing me to meet the divine. The divine has no face. When I met this omnipotent presence I was in awe, full of love. The time was ready for me to come back and I adamantly screamed and said no, I did not want to go back. Then, the angels lifted me up and I heard the sound "swoosh, swoosh" and I knew I would be fine. I woke up from this healing inside the room where my friend Susan Lee was giving me a Reiki healing massage session. My world was turned upside down. I knew my purpose here and never again would I doubt what my life is all about.

That experience in the Akashic fields grounded myself and directed me to what my passion is: bringing others back to their home.

Before I started my studies with the Akashic Records, I heard this voice from my guides, **"you are returning home."** I thought for a moment there that I was going to die. I did not realize that my home is my soul's home. Tapping into the most amazing book of my life, I was able to see my soul's highest potential and mission here on earth. This became my passion to teach, helping others see their book of lives, to heal our deepest wounds and to know that we are always protected, guided and loved.

"May your Akashic Records lighten up your soul's path. May the sparks of the Divine light of the Akashic Records permeate your cellular level of consciousness and memories, to remember your soul's home."

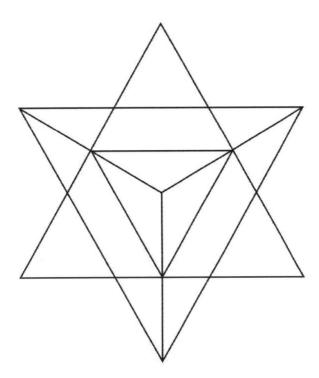

Channeled Messages

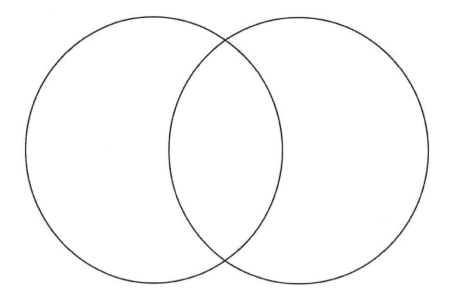

Waking up with the Masters

The divine infinite intelligence of the creator is within us in our multi-dimensional bodies of light and love. Our cellular fibers, tissues, membranes, bio-etheric fields, crystalline fields, holographic matrices, memories, and consciousness hold these energetic blueprints of the Divine Source of all that is. We have forgotten the codes and keys to unlock this wisdom. Right now these graces are being dispensed to humanity. We are at the threshold of the awakening of our divine consciousness. We are blessed to be in this divine field of creation. Our portals are opening and accelerating as we awaken as a whole collective consciousness.

The body, mind and heart consciousness of our humanity is shifting into being divine. The masks that we wear can lead us astray from what our truth is. The illusions that blind us, the sense of separation, can get in the way of achieving the mastery of our soul's purpose.

The sacred fire of the Holy Spirit resides in the sacred heart and burns away our darkness. Let us create space for the infusion of light. This sacred heart space is where we want to ground our monkey mind.

This is where we step into the sacred dance with the Divine. The fire within our sacred hearts ignites our passion to co-create a life filled with grace and divine eternal love.

By opening our Akashic Records, we master our soul's purpose: Being a Cosmic Soul. The truth that resides in every one of us will open the hidden portals. These open doors reveal clarity, precision and understanding why things happen, particularly in the dark night of our soul.

What are the treasures hidden in our darkness? How can we see the light in these situations and find the courage to empower ourselves? What are the steps to liberate our attachments from these blockages? What is true freedom? What are the secrets of the Masters that may answer our overwhelming challenges? These questions expand our consciousness and bring light into our realities.

Truth. What is our truth? Truth is relative and different for every one of us. We hold the blueprints to our destinies. We can only align to our personal truth when we are broken open. Our souls hold the keys to our truth when we are able to let go of control and surrender to the divine flow of our calling. When there is no resistance, we flow with divine grace. This is the true calling of the spiritual warrior. We are being called to let go of our ego and merge to the grand design of our blueprints.

The Akashic Records hold our soul's vibrations. We align to our truth when we can access our blueprints. This will give us a glimpse of our future ascended mastery. We are here to co-create this divine plan, interweaving with all other sentient beings.

What is the liberation of our spirit?

In liberation, the Self is free from the attachments of this world. This allows us to be free from the chains of human deceptions, from lies and manipulations. It is these trappings that hinder us from being a master.

Mastery is an alchemical process; we are turning lead into gold through our spiritual wisdom. The illusions of being separated from the Source are the ego's way of tricking us that we are small. We are bigger than what we think. How to transform these insecurities? We need to be observant of all of our creations. Everything that we see is our projection. Our perceptions are the magnet of our realities.

Our triggers invite us to go within and see what is blocking us. What did we create? First and foremost, we need to know we have the tools to think things through. Our mind will not have the solution to our shift. As we know that the same mind that created the situations is not capable of the alchemical process. The secret is to turn it around. When you think this reality is how it looks like, stop and pause, reflect and bring in another perception from the opposite of the spectrum.

Turn things around just like the Sufi twirls, go with the dance of the universal energy. Turn fear into love and light. Light and Love collapses the densities of any situations. Forgiveness is a superpower to see beyond the challenges. We can only go through that sacred space when we have purified our mind, heart, spirit and soul. The process of liberating our thoughts from false identification (ego), takes a deeper understanding of how our consciousness works.

When we attain freedom from our illusions, we become free spirited sentient beings of Light and Love. This sacred space is attained when one sees everything through the eyes of God. We will never attain inner peace as long as we perceive or blame others for our situations. We have to free ourselves from this idea, look within and know that others are the catalyst to empower us. They are simply mirrors. Every challenge contains a gem seeking to be found!

We have the power to transform what is on our plate with the assistance of the Ascended Masters, Archangels and angels, Benevolent beings of Light, our spiritual teams and guides, loved ones, ancestors from other dimensions and the Lords of the Akashic Records. The pathway to true freedom is becoming a Master of Light and Love.

Our soul mastery is about the integration of all shadow and light aspects to become wholesome. There are sacred contracts we have co-created in our blueprints that need clarity and understanding in order to fully function as the archetypal energy of a Master. When we understand the soul's perspective of what is our highest good in this incarnation, we will be fully aligned to our fate and destiny. The universe will synchronize our movements and bring us the fruits of our works. Miraculously, we will be basking in the sacred space of total surrender to God or the universe. The activations we are receiving from these Masters of Light and Love will bring us to our highest vibrational frequencies. The law of attraction will manifest right here, right now. Together with the creator, we will create this amazing dance of creation, manifesting our heart's desires and soul's purpose.

The Hologram of Our Souls

Observe where you are, become a witness of your emotions. Are you coming from fear and separation, or love? Our emotions can detect if we are aligned to our Higher Self. How are your mental thoughts? Are they positive or negative? Our mental thoughts are the barometer to know if we are vibrating in high frequency or not. How are your Chakra energy centers? Are they clear and open? If they are blocked, the energy within you can create physical illness. How are your dreams? They help us receive information regarding our psyche and astral travels. Scan your consciousness, to help you align with your Higher Self.

What is the Higher Self?

The Higher Self is the hologram of our Soul that can manifest the best version of our selves here in our incarnated body. When we are aligned to our Soul, we live in our creative expression. We are in the space of inner connectivity with all that is. The universe of our soul is where all the stars and planets align, creating a symphony of the language of our creation.

Our body systems are like these planets, they need to communicate in harmony for our highest good. If they are not in sync, they will let us know by showing up as physical symptoms.

Our body parts are interrelated with our emotions, mental thoughts and energy. Everything is interconnected. The force field that holds this body is the Holy Spirit which is a spark from the creation of all that is. The I Am presence that we are is the sacred space that bonds or glues us to the Source or God of light. When we are awake, we are aware of this magnificent luminous presence.

How can we get to this space of connectivity?

To attain this space of connectivity, we have to be aware of the information that we are interpreting and assimilating in our complex systems. This information takes space, time, and energy in our multi-dimensional selves. We are fractals of the micro-cosm of the universe. Every little fragment or aspect of our being, namely mental, emotional, etheric and astral bodies, must be in unison with our Higher Self. These vibrations will create a force field that will resist anything that is not vibrating with our Higher Self.

To simplify and ground this information, let us look at an example in a relationship with another person where you felt abandoned. Ask yourself, and reflect, why are you feeling this way? Where is this coming from? Journal with your Akashic Records and you find out that the root of abandonment is your relationship with your father. Now, you can release this and ask the Masters of Light to help you transmute this energy in your system. Invoke **St. Germain and the Violet Flame** to help you clear abandonment in all timelines, dimensions, space and reality. Ask **Archangel Chamuel** to infuse the pink light in your heart chakra for unconditional love to flow into all your systems.

We are never alone. We have the Ascended Masters, Archangels and angels, spiritual teams and guides, benevolent beings of light and loved ones to assist us in connecting to our Higher Selves. By being conscious and invoking them in our presence, we create a strong force field in all our creations. Be aware, awake, align and activate your universal self with the Masters of Light.

The Genesis of Creation

We are the Masters of Light, incarnated in this physical dimension. We are now in the ascension process of our spirit and our Soul is reaching enlightenment, the golden state of our Light. We are here to simplify the genesis of creation, starting from the Akasha, which is the field of primordial substance; where everything in our collective consciousness is created before it becomes a form in our third dimension.

This wisdom is transmitted through the channels of our **Council of Light** to assist humanity in understanding what their creations are coming from and how they can assist us in our ascension process.

What is ascension?

It is a process in which our spirit that lies within our physical body transcends the victim consciousness and memories of our DNA, bloodline, ancient lineage, holographic matrices, bio-ethereal fields, cellular tissues, membranes, molecular and energetic level of existence are being harmonized into higher frequencies of Light. Our emotions are calibrated by the frequency of vibrations that we are resonating with. If we are vibrating in lower levels and below the frequency of Light fields which are the negative and shadow frequency, we will be creating the same resonance of experience. Negativity and shadows attract suffering and pain. Therefore, if our consciousness emits a higher frequency of vibration we then experience and attract positive and loving situations. Light attracts Light. We are Light beings within our physical, mental, emotional, etheric and astral body.

Our Soul is the hologram of all our bodies in the multi-dimensions that we traverse. We are confined within this physical body but our Soul is expansive and it travels when we are asleep and reach the Alpha, Theta and Delta state of our brain waves. This is the unconscious and we are being called to be conscious of our multi-dimensional selves. The Super conscious state of our existence is the fractal of God particles or the Source of all that is. The Creator, creation and co-creators is us existing in one unified consciousness, which is the zero point field of creation. Our science and spirituality is one, the human mind cannot simplify the creation because it is functioning in the egoic mind which has no power in the universal mind of God or creator. We are powerless human beings if we are not conscious of the magnificent Universal mind of God, whoever God is for you.

How do we connect to the Universal mind of God or creator?

Our brain, which is composed of left and right brain hemispheres, needs to attune to the higher frequencies of Light with the Masters. Integrate, align and be activated by our Higher Selves. Our Kundalini Light that lies within the coccyx, spinal vertebra, and central nervous system are connected to the Light of the Cosmic portal and the universal energy. When the Pineal, Hypothalamus and Pituitary glands are activated, it literally diffuses the energetic blockages and transcends this unconscious state of mind to the super conscious fields of our consciousness.

How do we stay balanced and grounded in this third dimension?

Our Soul taps into the pinnacle of our co-creator state of mind; we become super conscious of all our creations. We become responsible and accountable for all our creations, thoughts, words, emotions and actions. We become the observer of our realities in the field of manifestation.

We become the Master of our true Light which is our Soul. Our multi-sensory faculties of receiving communication is heightened and attuned to the frequencies of Light. We are the transmitters of the messages that we are receiving from all benevolent beings of Light. We are the channel and vehicle of information towards truth, love and light.

Our body Deva spirit that holds the blueprint of our human species as incarnation in the third dimension animates our actions. Our Higher Self, which is our Soul that is expansive and infinitesimal, holds the blueprint for our manifestation.

They need to be integrated in the energetic fields to harmonize, communicate effectively what the body's spirit and Soul wants to create in this lifetime. We need to call them in the energetic fields to harmonize and collaborate for our highest good and healing. Once done, we become one in unison with our spirit and Soul. The Higher Self relays Light encoded information and knowledge to the spirit and the self-integrates with the true Self which is the Higher Self. The shadow and light are being integrated in our cellular level of memories and consciousness in all timelines, dimension, space and reality. We now begin the journey of the ascended Soul. We are multi-dimensional light beings and we are given the access to our Akashic Records to consciously create and harmonize our energetic fields.

Nature is our natural healer, because we are encoded with the elemental factors of nature. The fire, earth, water, air and ether are fragments of our existence. When we become conscious beings of Light we become attuned to our Mother Earth. The genesis of creation is returning to us with Light encoded frequencies. The consciousness of our Ascended Masters as Lord Jesus, Lord Buddha, Goddess Isis, Mother Mary, Quan Yin, Goddess Lakshmi and many others that we receive guidance from are here in our eternal space. The secret code to creation is to ask. "**Ask and you shall receive**" Simple yet so profound.

When we ask, we are receiving messages and we attract situations that will conspire to our pure intentions. The Universe is a field of intelligence; we have the power to co-exist with the Masters of Light by simply opening our mind and hearts to the vibratory frequency of love and light. Create a life that makes a difference in this dimension to assist humanity in our ascension process. Our Souls have lived in many lifetimes and we are amazingly here to co-exist in this energy field of creation. You are a Master of Light, remembering your eternal home. You are a part of the collective consciousness of transformation, death and rebirth of our Mother Earth into the paradise of Genesis.

your Life Story?

In this lifetime we find it difficult to separate ourselves from the stories that we co-create in the universe. As observers of our stories, we can find the treasures in the darkness. The veil in our Third Eye Chakra is so thick that we cannot see the bigger picture, perhaps of why things that are not so good happen to us. We believe the stories that we create because we were pre-conditioned as human beings to believe what we see and have forgotten that there is more to what we can see. This physical reality is only the surface of what is deeper in the mysterious life that we live.

How can we get out of our victim consciousness roles? How do we empower ourselves? When we see others as separate from us, we are still running in the egoic mode. That means we have not developed our sense of unified consciousness, which is about being one with everything that we co-create. Our projections are our mirrors of what is inside us. So we need to understand that our enemies so to speak are actually us reflecting what we need to shift in order for us to be wholesome.

We are here to experience dichotomy, fear and love. What are you choosing? Let go of the story of your victimhood and wake up to your empowered self. We can shift our perceptions and consciousness into being one with others. When we accept our part and responsibility for creating the story, then we know for sure, that we co-create whatever is in our fields. Are we ready to see the truth for what it is? As long as we see others separated from us, we will not see the gifts in the stories that we had agreed to with our Sacred Contracts. Open your heart, wake up to the catalysts of your stories. Let forgiveness be the key in your heart and soul to allow miracles to unfold in your lives.

Our stories are written in our blueprints of the Akashic Records. When we align with this luminous Akashic field, we will find light to direct us into our greatness and magnificent paths of our souls. To get to this lighted path we need to know and understand that there are laws in the universe that we go through and when we are not aligned with these laws, we are lost in the darkness, the dark night of our soul.

Tools to guide us in our souls' purpose:

1. Your story serves your soul's purpose.

2. Name the theme of your victim consciousness. Shift this into empowerment. Forgive the catalyst for the story to unfold into its greatness.

3. Start where you are, everything will shift when you put attention to the lighter side of life.

4. Everything passes away, let go of attachments to your story as a victim. You have the power to shift this into your victorious story. Let go of pain and allow healing to manifest.

5. The lighter you are, the easier it gets. FAITH is total surrender to the unknown.

6. Everything is impermanent and uncertain. How we see ourselves as victims will transform if we let go of our attachment. You are here to find the gifts of your victim consciousness.

7. You are never alone and never separated from the Divine creative force of creations. Co-create your victorious life and TRUST that you are on the right path to your ascension process.

8. Everything is energy; choose your vibrations towards love and light. Fear is constrictive and will not lead you into your expansion.

9. Surround yourself with light hearted, compassionate, kind and caring people who will support you with your growth. Let go of others that are not for you. Have clear boundaries and respect for yourself.

10. Know that you are always guided. The Masters of Light are with you, call them and ask for blessings and you shall receive.

What is your Soul's Destiny?

This is a profound question because we are multi-dimensional beings of Light. There are limitless and boundless ways that we can choose, which path to take. The blueprints of our souls, the Akashic Records, can illuminate the path as they are our guideposts to our destination. The Akashic Records give us clarity to what we need to focus on and what to let go of.

When we follow our chosen path, we fly with the wings of the wind. This takes us to the pinnacle of the mountain top, looking over the majestic view of our creations. This vast expanse encompasses all sentient beings that are part of our Akashic contracts and manifests all creations with the Source of all that is.

We are born with gifts, blessings that we receive from our Creator or Source we can call God or any kind of higher power that stands for you. In our journeys, we can get lost because of our ego and fear. We are in the collective consciousness of humanity that includes shadow and light perspectives of our existence. We may forget how to navigate and activate our souls to live this lifetime in harmonious and synchronized movements with the universe.

We are a part of the grand design of the Creator. Our soul's journeys are patterns and designs that are interweaving with each other to be able to see the bigger picture of our existence. Our goal is to examine our patterns, woven together in intricate layers and complicated details, with our multi-dimensional state of being. Our mastery lies in understanding the entanglements and patterns that we keep repeating so we can flow with the Universal energy.

Masters are investigators, deeply delving into the mystical laws of the Universal and Cosmic energy. We are here to experience all the creations that we have tapped into from all timelines, dimensions and realities. Thus, we create a better understanding of why we are here. Hence, we can share with others this illuminating Light from the Source.

We have to understand our soul's journey from nothingness to physical reality and back around. We go to nothingness when we pass on from this dimension. Our soul's eternal state is a full completion of the circle of life with the Source of all creations. Our souls are eternally present in the past and future lives. We are in this quantum soup of our collective consciousness. We can change the past, travel to the future of endless probabilities. However, the present choices will master our soul's destiny.

Our Akashic Records hold the soul's vibration of infinite and timeless existence. We can open, download information, unblock impediments and heal. We can release unnecessary clutter and shadows of the soul. We can bring pure awareness to our existence and our soul's crystal clear perspective of our destiny.

THE AKASHIC RECORDS

What are the Akashic Records?

Akashic Records are our sacred soul's living library. Here in the etheric fields of the Akasha where the primordial substance of all that is, has been recorded. In Sanskrit, the word Akasha means ether, sky or primordial substance before anything in the universe becomes a form. The universal energy in this realm manifests what is in store in the blueprints of our souls. Everything that is seen in our physical dimension has blueprints in the Akashic fields. Our soul progresses into each timeline, dimension and reality that we created and manifested, leaving energetic substance or imprints in our soul's consciousness.

Akashic Records are a living library of your soul or the blueprint of your book of life. Everything is recorded in your soul's Records; all your thoughts, emotions, words, and actions in all timelines, dimensions and realities. Can you imagine the vastness of this all? It is also the Records of all sentient beings, any experiences that happened in our collective consciousness. These Records are alive, interactive and you can rewrite what is written when you tap into and open your own Records. It is very sacred because it is the vibration of your soul. There are gatekeepers or Record keepers that hold the keys to let you in and unlock your book of life.

You receive activations and empowerment from the Akashic Masters when you are in your Records. They are beings of light that give powers that will transform your ordinary state of human consciousness into an empowered state of divine oneness. The healing that takes place is very powerful and transformational. It heals blockages from all timelines, dimensions and realities.

Tapping into the Akashic Records is the highest form of healing in all mankind. We can tap into the resources and informational data bank of the universal library of our collective consciousness. Every illness or disease has an energetic imprint in our soul's data bank. Therefore, we can create the shift in this field and have the soul's perspective on why things are happening to us. We can understand and gain clarity on how we can make the best alternative approach for our condition.

What are the lessons of our souls?

We can witness our highest potential and create miracles along the way. When we are aligned with our blueprints, we can realize the truth of our existence. What are the important things that we should focus our attention on so we can live peaceful and happy lives?

The vibrations of the Akashic Records purify us as fire in our souls. Like diamonds, we are being tested and purified to have that brilliance of our Light shine into the world. The Phoenix comes out from the ashes to give rise to the freedom of our confinement which are the trappings of the ego.

We can only recognize the attachments when we awaken and become free from all the illusions of the humanity's collective consciousness. We have to undergo purification to fully embody the illuminating Light of the Source of everything.

Illusions are the shadows of our spirit. See them as the gateway or portals to open us into a new dimension of understanding how oneness can sustain in our existence. The shadows are part of this consciousness because we are here to integrate these shadows into our light.

When fully integrated, we become one with everything. There are no hindrances to what we can create and what can manifest in our energy fields. We hold the keys to unlock the codes of our Akashic Records.

The clarity and purity will be given to us when we ask the Lords of the Akashic Records. They are the gatekeepers of these libraries of our souls. They can give access to the book of life of each one of us incarnated here to experience what it is to be human in this timeline.

As we traverse these lifetimes, our souls collect energetic imprints from all lifetimes that we have lived. All thoughts, words, emotions and actions are recorded in our book of life. These halls of Light hold the vibrational imprints of all that had been created, omnipresent and future lives of our collective consciousness.

We are tapping into the unconscious, sub-conscious and super conscious summation of our existence since we have separated from the Source of all that is. When we came here, our consciousness chose this timeline to recreate oneness. It is like returning home.

Our home is our soul's vibrational frequency. We attune to the universal and cosmic light that we are. Then, we become universal conscious selves, meaning we know that our existence here is bigger than what we think it is.

We shift in our evolution of consciousness and become free spirits in our conscious choices. We become the observer of our lifetimes. We now have the power to see beyond the veil. In fact, there is no more veil of separation for those who can see beyond this form of illusion.

We become one in no space and time; we become omnipresent, omnipotent and omniscient beings of light and love. We become pure in thoughts and words, emotions are resonating in a higher frequency of love and light and our actions are consciously chosen to release others from harm. We become free of karma and abide by the laws of the universe. These are the fruits of tapping into the Akashic Records.

Life becomes fruitful, happy and simple. We become clear conduits or channels of love and light messages. These are the evident results of being a master of your soul. Opening and consulting your Records gives you the soul's perspective of this incarnation.

It is a process to attain this mastery. When you know that you have no attachments to this world and travel lightly with joy, compassion, love and peace in your heart, you have attained freedom and liberation from this incarnation. You become a radiating light for others to see and to remember their own luminosity.

Let us consciously love others as ourselves. See others as our reflections in our complexities as human beings. Let us share compassion and kindness to all sentient beings. Let the Light shine upon our hearts and our souls magnify our existence in our daily moments. Be attuned to our Akashic Records and receive the graces and blessings of these wondrous compendium vibrations of our souls.

What are the blockages in our Akashic Records?

We are conditioned from the past within our collective victim consciousness. These are energetic imprints from all timelines, dimensions, space and realities that we had created in our Akashic fields. Our family, bloodlines, and DNA carried this into our energetic fields.

Our karmic bondages from the past, attachments and cords, contracts, vows or agreements, drains and hooks, entities or souls that are attached to our energy fields, emotional traumas, constrictions and injuries, these are some of the blockages that we need to release and receive the grace of the Source of all that is.

When we become aware of our blockages, our awareness transcends our victim consciousness. We will find ourselves not reacting anymore to conflicts or chaos. We receive clarity, information, knowledge, wisdom and healing from the Masters of Light. These are called activations, attunements, and empowerment from these powerful Masters, beings of Light.

Being Conscious of our Karmic Effect

In this lifetime, we are experiencing darkness and shadows of the past. Our ancestors, bloodlines, DNA, and our collective unconscious have passed this unto us. We are here to transcend the effects of karma. We can support each other, by being compassionate and kind to each other. We cannot sustain this world that we live in with fear and pain. We are here to commune and coalesce the truth beyond our illusions. Love and light is our power, we are being supported by the Masters of Light in this transition of our collective consciousness. The evolution is within and when we reach the pinnacle of our enlightenment, we have arrived. We return home, to our soul's purpose.

The blueprint is within us like the seeds in a lotus flower. It keeps the wisdom within until it is time to radiate the beauty. It radiates its beauty in the midst of a muddy foundation. Our light can only shine when we are integrated with our divinity. The power of our source of life is through this soulful energy, the spark that keeps us in light.

Do not be consumed with the external force of materialism. It is not our truth. Our true power is our divine Self.

What is Karma?

These are patterns of energy that link us to past lives. The seed of our present lifetime has an energetic imprint from these past lives in our book of life. We can see these patterns in our behavior that keep repeating in our lives. There are themes of behavior like addiction and abandonment. There are energetic imprints in our Akashic Records that we need to see, to reveal to us the connection in our current lifetime from the past. In knowing our karma, we are able to ask for help to clear it in our present lifetime. Every thought, intention, word, emotion, and action that we do creates cause and effect. These are vibrations of our souls that are recorded in our Akashic Records.

We are living in challenging times. Tremendous chaos surrounds us. What can we do to alleviate the pain of our human consciousness? We have to be conscious of our own weaknesses, karma, bondage, blockages, hooks, cords, and temptations. Without knowing our own shadows, we are unable to pinpoint what areas need light.

We have freewill. We can opt for either light or darkness. If we do not wake up in this incarnation, we are going to continue living in the wheel of karma. Our patterns are not going to shift. We are perpetuating the same suffering in our collective unconscious. It is time to rise up, take the lead, and have the courage to move forward. Have faith and totally surrender to our calling. Heed the call and start to see the signs around us.

The doors are open; the veils are lifted for those who seek. Allow the spiritual Masters of Light to reside in our hearts. They have been calling our name. We are the gift to the universe. Our time is here to shine our light. Burn away all the shadows that impede our ascension. When we are ready and done, we will begin a journey of rebirth like the phoenix that rises up from the burnt ashes. Transformation takes purification from all aspects of our being. Integrity is our arrow, where we focus our attention. Know that we are always guided, protected, and loved.

We cannot move forward if we keep our attachment to the material world. Let us let go and surrender our expectations to the outcome. Fear is crippling. We are stronger than our fears. Imagine clearing the mind of thoughts that do not serve us. Ill feelings about our neighbors are only going to create more toxicity in our energy systems.

Be an observer of your consciousness. Is it calibrating with love and light? Or is it vibrating in envy, anger, jealousy, separation, and resentment? The latter are clear signs that we are in the midst of toxicity. Be aware, recognize the fear, and clear these away. With the help of healers and assistance from the Masters of Light we can cleanse all these toxic energies.

Prayer:

"Divine Source of love and light, we ask to clear, release, and heal our karmic effects on all other sentient beings that we have caused harm consciously and unconsciously. We ask for compassion, forgiveness, mercy and kindness to rewire our neural pathways, patterns and create a new rebirth of our consciousness.

May our intentions uphold the truth of love and light, we now ask to receive these blessings and gifts of empowerment, inner peace, love, bliss, abundance, joy, and success in all aspects of our lives. Thank you, thank you, thank you, and so it is. Please seal this prayer with the sacred Merkabah."

Breathe, Forgive and Let Go

We are multi-dimensional beings of light and love. When we are going through some changes, we have to know that we have the space to breathe and remember why we are here. Our breath anchors us to our body. Our thoughts are busy creating thoughts from the past imprints in our sub-conscious and unconscious mind. Our hearts are busy feeling our emotions. We then get caught in the busyness of their functions. We forget to breathe and remember that this is our home. We breathe and anchor our thoughts and emotions into this space of stillness. This creates the gap between chaos and feelings.

Forgiveness is the path to feeling lighter about our buried emotions from the past. When we forgive, we let go of the toxic heaviness in our Heart Chakra. This is the way to release the stress that is created unconsciously when we hold onto feelings that are toxic. You can say this forgiveness prayer, "I forgive those people who have hurt me and I forgive myself for hurting others consciously and unconsciously in all timelines, dimensions, space, and realities and so it is." Envision these people that you had hurt and those that had hurt you. Stay and feel this in your heart.

You can co-create a new reality for yourself when you align to the universal energies. By opening and clearing your Chakra energy systems you are able to align and receive these amazing energies from the universe. You have assistance from the Ascended Masters and angels. You are never alone in this soul's journey. They are here to help you transcend the victim consciousness and become empowered by the love and light that is bestowed upon us. All the things that matter to you are honored and blessed. You are the co-creator of the Source of all that is. You are gifted in many ways by believing that and having a strong faith; you will be able to tread the waters on this vast ocean of love. Breathe, forgive, and co-create a new life with the Source of all that is.

Masters Of Light

Who are the Masters of Light?

The Masters of Light are Ascended Masters, Benevolent beings of Light that are here to help us in our ascension process, to raise the frequency of our collective vibrations and to help us master our soul's purpose. They are here to support and guide us to our highest potential.

Our highest potential in this lifetime is to experience love with all. This is oneness. Receiving activations and empowerment from these Masters is a very powerful spiritual tool to help us transcend our human condition. They work miracles in our lifetime and bring us into a space of sacredness, inner peace, surrender, serendipity, fulfillment, happiness, abundance, love, joy and bliss. We need to build relationships with them just like a friendship. We have to ask for their help and intervention. Increase our knowledge with their mastery and we can access their presence anytime we want. Because everything is energy, there is no time and space. We are eternal souls like them. If we can work from this wisdom, we will be master alchemists of our destiny.

There are a lot of spiritual guides that you can call when you are creating a sacred space for your Akashic Records healing. They are with you to assist you in your healing. They are here to give you messages, clarity and understanding on what is happening in your current situation. These guides have mastery and special gifts. Knowing them will help you in knowing who to call and create a relationship with. While I open the Akashic Records, I call on these guides to help me attain a clear reading and understanding on the messages. We are the channels of light and love. We are the messengers to help others remember who they truly are. Each one of us has this innate healing ability when we are open and trusting in the divine intervention.

List of the Masters of Light:

Archangel Metatron– Metatron is the scribe of the Akashic Records; he takes notes on all our thoughts, words, emotions and actions in all timelines. We ask to open the stellar gateway and the cosmic diamond portal from the heavens to activate our **Merkabah** (divine vehicle of light) and attune us to our Akashic Records. Clearing all our Chakra energy centers and anchoring our golden light in Mother Earth Gaia to help us open and rewrite our Records.

Archangel Michael and the Blue Ray- Call on Michael for protection and cutting the cords and attachments from people, places and things that do not serve our highest good. He is also the one to call to heal our Throat Chakra for expressing our authentic self, will and choices. Before attempting to speak with others especially in conflicts, create this bonding and call Michael for assistance to help you open up more and be vulnerable with your emotions to go deeper.

Archangel Raziel- Call Raziel for spiritual understanding, clairvoyance and to know the secrets of God. He holds the keys to the kingdom of the creations. I ask for the sacred geometrical form to infuse us with healing and to seal the Akashic Records with these symbols. Visualize these symbols when you are closing the Records and see these stamps in the pages of the Records.

Archangel Chamuel- Archangel Chamuel heals the heart Chakra, to release and clear any toxins around the energy fields, to melt down all the walls and barriers around the heart, and to infuse the pink light of healing, unconditional love, peace, and forgiveness.

Archangel Ariel- Archangel Ariel helps for the provision of our material needs. We have the birthright to receive abundance and prosperity as we follow our intuition and accept the gifts that we are given. Accept and believe that we are gifted with intuition, clarity and understanding. Use this wisdom and know that we deserve the gift of money that we will receive as a gift for our service of healing. Have the courage to move forward and express our truth, to follow our heart and manifest our dreams to come true.

Archangel Raphael and the Green Ray– Archangel Raphael heals our body, mind, heart, spirit and soul. He takes care of all our needs; trust that we are safe, secure and loved. We are a vehicle and beacon of light serving as a messenger of love and light for others to know that they are loved. We can give our worries to the angels and believe that they will take care of our needs. Have faith and trust that all things are well. Let go of any expectations from the outcome but totally surrender to the unknown.

St. Germain and the Violet Flame- Invoke St. Germain for the transmutation of energy that is not of light. Ask him to clear and release anything that is not serving our highest good, any attachments, negative entities, souls, cords, hooks, drains, unconscious negative thoughts, patterns, conditions from our DNA, memories and consciousness. We ask that these energies go back to the Source of love and light.

Lord Jesus Christ- Call on Jesus for forgiveness and compassion. To forgive our enemies who are simply catalysts for change, Jesus helps us see the bigger picture of why things had to happen between us. Say this forgiveness prayer, "I forgive myself consciously and unconsciously for hurting others. I forgive others for hurting me consciously and unconsciously in all timelines, dimensions, space and reality." This will help us heal our unconscious thoughts, words, emotions and actions that we did in past lives as well. Forgiving will make us feel lighter and free us from any burden that we are carrying in our energetic fields.

Medicine Buddha– Call on the Medicine Buddha for enlightenment and healing of our mind, body, heart and spirit. He gives us wisdom and clarity to know the difference, to have compassion and kindness towards ourselves and others. Through him we expand in love for our brothers and sisters in our community. Doing no harm, we gain inner peace and truly become at one with the universe.

Lord Melchizedek- Lord Melchizedek hears the call for wisdom, clarity and support. When I first met Melchizedek, it was such a strong force that I was not able to move and get up from lying on the floor. Ever since then, I called for his help with supporting me in my work. He was my ascension teacher to help me with increasing my light frequency.

Mother Mary- Call on Mother Mary for nurturing your heart and healing your inner child. She sends warmth, comforting and lovingly energy to guide you on your path. When there is brokenness of twin flames she helps soothe your brokenness.

Goddess Quan Yin- Quan Yin uplifts your spirit. Call on her for relief from your sorrows. She takes away your grief and places it in her vessel of love. She has a lot of wisdom and compassionate guidance. Listen to her voice touching your heart and allow her to come and take away your sorrows.

Goddess Isis- Call upon Isis for your goddess energy, remembering that you truly are a goddess of feminine divine love. When you are lost in your partnership, unable to feel worthy and valued, ask for her assistance. She can fill your heart with empowerment and give assurance that you are divine within. Feel her grace by completely opening your heart and receive love from her presence.

Master Paramahansa Yogananda- Invoke him for mastery of manifestation, inner peace and wisdom. He connected with me in Los Angeles and literally guided me to teach

Mastery of Akashic Records, while I was being guided to visit his lovely retreat center. This was an amazing experience that I never imagined, that I was guided by this beautiful Master of light.

Crystal Devas, fairies, and elementals- Call these beautiful beings in the elemental fields to assist you in manifestation, connections and healing your elemental physical body. They have the secret ingredients of our third dimension. They give us joy like children of the earth. They present us with lightness, healing and clear guidance.

The List of the Seven Chohans and Archangels in our Chakra Energy Systems

We ask these Ascended Masters and Archangels to assist us in our Chakra Energy Centers when we are clearing, releasing and healing our energy vortexes.

Crown Chakra- We ask Ascended Master Lanto and Archangel Jophiel with the Yellow Ray for wisdom, enlightenment and judgment.

Third Eye Chakra- We ask Ascended Master Hilarion and Archangel Raphael with the Green Ray for truth, vision and prosperity.

Throat Chakra- We ask Ascended Master El Morya and Archangel Michael with the Blue Ray for willpower, expression and speaking the truth.

Heart Chakra- We ask Ascended Master Paul the Venetian and Archangel Chamuel with the Pink Ray for love, forgiveness and beauty.

Solar Plexus Chakra- We ask Ascended Master Lady Nada and Archangel Uriel with the Purple and Golden Ray for peace, service and brotherhood.

Sacral Chakra- We ask the Ascended Master St. Germaine and Archangel Zadkiel with the Violet ray for transmutation, compassion and forgiveness.

Root Chakra- We ask the Ascended Master Serapis Bey and Archangel Gabriel with the White Ray for messages, purity and discipline.

We can ask them to come in meditation and upon opening our Akashic Records, to send us messages and help us in healing, clearing and releasing our energy centers. These Masters of Light come when you call them just like friends, they are here communicating and helping us in our transitions to receiving more light and love from our Akashic Records. They give information on how we can shift our perceptions and consciousness into being divinely guided and supported by these celestial beings of light.

Prayer to Archangel Michael

Imagine this beautiful blue light around you, the Blue Ray. Feel a blue cloak around you, warmth and comforting, a blanket around your shoulders, neck and back. Visualize Archangel Michael standing in front of you carrying his blue sword with his armored chest. He is a very strong and powerful force of light. We now ask Archangel Michael to cut any cords, attachments, entanglements, shadows that do not calibrate in light, to cast away any entities that are attached to our souls, to cut the cords of ropes around our neck that have suffocated us in other timelines, universes, other planets and stars.

We ask Archangel Michael to cut any energetic cords of sadness, grief and anger that we may have been suffering from because we have not accepted ourselves. We ask Archangel Michael to free us from suppression and give us freedom. Give us this beautiful endearment that opens our hearts and allows us to speak our truth, truth that purifies our hearts and souls.

Give us the Light that will make us feel loved, heal and clear our thoughts in all cellular levels of memory and consciousness. Please, bring your blue light around our brain cells, tissues and membranes and bring sparks to our electrical neural-pathways that will activate light and joy. Please bring us back to paradise where the angels are playing, bring us home where we feel loved and safe, and seal every crevice of our existence with this beautiful blue Light. Help us shed every darkness and shadow attached to us. We now cast all these negative energies that we no longer need, sending them back to the source of love and light.

Envision Archangel Michael standing in front of you handing his Blue Light Sword, and he commands, "And now, you are free, always protected and loved!" Thank you, thank you, thank you. And so it is. "

Accessing Our Akashic Records

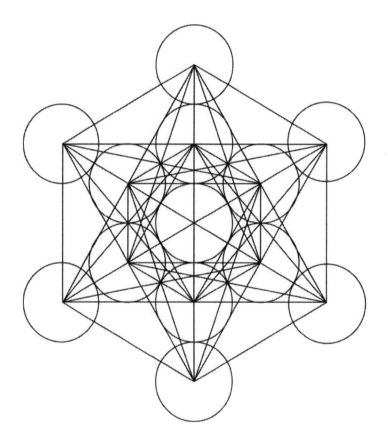

How can we access our Akashic Records?

There are a lot of portals to enter the Akashic fields. They can be accessed via dreams, intuitions, meditation or when you are in the zone, perhaps, creating art or music, but you may be unconscious about it. The access that we use, through a sacred prayer, directly communicates with your Soul or Higher Self.

Journaling with the Akashic Records

We rewrite the things that are not serving our highest good. Before we can access our Records, there are portals that we have to traverse. One portal is gone through the forgiveness prayer. We have to forgive ourselves and others from unconscious and conscious thoughts, and from actions that are harming us. Forgiveness encompasses all timelines, dimensions and realities.

Then, we have to clear blockages that do not benefit our energy field and moreover, interfere with our access. A sacred prayer then can invoke our Akashic Masters or the Lords of the Akashic Records to open our book and allow us access to our Akashic Records. It is but proper to close our Records after the consultation and healing.

What are the benefits of accessing the Akashic Records?

We receive attunements, activations and empowerment from the Akashic fields. Consulting our Records brings clarity and direction to our path. We receive spiritual guidance and tools to shift our victim consciousness. We become empowered and know that we are always guided and supported. It brings abundance, miracles and synchronicities in this lifetime. We become multi- dimensional and align to our highest potential. This healing connects us to our soul family and allows us to vibrate at our highest potential.

The vibrations of the Akashic fields hasten the evolution of our soul. We are spurred towards growth and our ascension process. They align us to our highest potential and to the highest good of all humanity. As we heal our mind, body, hearts and souls' Records, we create a rippling effect through the collective consciousness. It allows others who are vibrating in lower emotional frequencies to receive these codes of light and they become attuned to their positive vibration.

Consulting the Akashic Records teaches the student to consciously open and work with their own soul's Records.

The following benefits are experienced:

- Clearing blockages from all timelines, dimensions, space and reality
- Acknowledging and knowing our unconscious negative beliefs, patterns and conditioning from ancient lineage, bloodline, and DNA
- Clearing our Chakra energy centers
- Bringing true forgiveness and compassion in our lifetime with all sentient beings
- Working with and having relationships with our Ascended Masters, Archangels and angels, spiritual team and guides, loved ones from other dimensions, your Higher Self and body deva spirit
- Taking steps and having the courage to move forward
- Healing unresolved issues and conflicts with others
- Finding our sacred gifts
- Transcending our victim consciousness

- Heightening our gifts such as clairvoyance, clairsentience, claircognizance, clairaudience

- Tapping into our highest potential and highest good of all sentient beings

- Clarity of our soul's purpose and personal direction

- Creating and manifesting infinite possibilities

- Deeper sense and relationship with the divine intelligence

- Knowing the Universal Laws

- Paradigm shift from Me to We spiritual integration

- Oneness with all sentient beings

- Remembering our incarnations and past lives consciously

- Having inner peace, abundance, bliss, love, and joy

Guidelines to Open your Akashic Records:

1. Don't consume any alcohol, recreational drugs or drive while you are in your Records. Create a safe and sacred space. Meditate and invoke your spiritual guides and loved ones.

2. Open your Records with full conscious mind, open eyes to avoid trance channeling. Be fully aware of

Your senses and environment.

3. Use your current legal name while opening your Records.

4. Make sure you are in a space of love and grace.

5. Create your intentions, list of questions to help you process what you want. Say your opening prayer and close the Records with the closing prayer.

6. Ground yourself after each reading, like drinking water, wash your face, eating something light or walking.

7. Be honest with yourself, even if the information doesn't make sense or you don't like what you are hearing.

8. Don't teach this to others without proper training.

9. Scan your body, mind, heart, spirit and surroundings when you open your Records.

10. Ask for protection when opening your Records.

Creating a Sacred Space

The spiritual tool of accessing your own Akashic Records is very sacred because you are tuning into your soul. Creating a sacred space is the first step in accessing your Records. The way I do it is like a ritual that I created. First, light a candle. Make sure you will be undisturbed by others, burn sage or Palo Santo to clear the space. Go through your meditative process, sitting comfortably with your eyes closed. Take deep breaths and go into your heart space.

Invoke the Masters of Light. Call **Archangel Metatron** to open the stellar gateway and the cosmic diamond portal. Ask for the activation of your Merkabah, the divine vehicle of light that links us to the divine blueprints of the Akashic Records. We ask to clear, release and heal all chakra energy centers.

Call **Archangel Michael** and the Blue Ray for protection, to cut any cords of attachments to places, things and people that are not serving your highest good. Call your Higher Self and body deva spirit to fully open and receive the angels light attunements and activations for our highest potential.

Call your spiritual guides, teams, loved ones and ancestors to support you in your healing and guide you for your highest good.

Call all the Ascended masters to help support your ascension process. Call **St. Germain and the Violet Flame** to transmute all energies that are not of light. Ask these energies to go back to the Source of all that is.

Call the benevolent beings of light to accelerate the frequency of light in your multi-dimensional bodies. Then, envision yourself in the Halls of the Library of the Akashic Records. Visualize yourself receiving your book of life and ask the Lords of the Akashic Records to open your book of life by stating your full name.

This is the password to your Records. Slowly envision your book opening with golden light around it. And say, **"The Records are now open, the Records are now open and the Records are now open."**

Ask questions and journal the answers. Whatever messages you receive, do not judge, resist or be scared. Let go of any and all expectations. After opening your Records, it is most important to close the Records.

Remember to close the Records! Say thank you three times to the Lords of the Akashic Records and ask that your records be closed. Say, **"The Records are now closed, the Records are now closed and the Records are now closed."**

Closing the Akashic Records is a very important part of the ritual. If you leave your records open for too long, you might feel physically sick. As a scribe, I open the Akashic

Records before I write, and there have been times when I've forgotten to close them and left it open. Once, I went back to bed, and felt nauseated. I asked myself: why am I feeling sick? I realized that I forgot to close the Records.

It can also cause dizziness, nausea, headaches and lightheadedness. After reading the Records, another important rule is grounding. Grounding can be a form of walking, earthing in nature, eating or having a salt bath for detoxification. Opening the Akashic Records can cause an imbalance in our neural pathways, so we need to ground to recharge with mother earth's magnetic fields. We receive a lot of cosmic Light and information that can over stimulate our system. Like electricity, we need to ground ourselves so we do not fry our brain wires.

Steps to Open your Heart and Akashic Records:

1. Create a sacred space for meditation. Light a candle. Meditate and invoke our Ascended Masters, Archangels, angels, spiritual guides and teams, gatekeepers, loved ones from other dimensions and our Higher Selves.

2. Open your Akashic Records and say this prayer, "I forgive consciously and unconsciously myself for hurting others. I forgive others consciously and unconsciously for hurting me, in all timelines, dimensions, space and reality." Feel that in your heart; put your right hand on your heart. Envision the faces of those you have hurt and those who have hurt you in this lifetime. Send them forgiveness, love and light. Ask Ascended Master Paul the Venetian and Archangel Chamuel to assist you in releasing unresolved issues and remnants of non-forgiveness in your heart chakra. Ask that you be infused with unconditional love, compassion, kindness and gentleness for yourself and others. Envision it is so, that it be done effortlessly, with ease, love and grace.

3. Say this release prayer, "I release any attachments, karmic bondage, beings, entities, souls, curses, hooks, drains, unconscious negative beliefs, patterns, conditioning from my ancient lineage and DNA. I ask these energies to transmute into the core of mother Earth Gaia and to go back to the Source of love and light to complete its soul's path. Be it done effortlessly, with ease, love and grace, and so it is."

4. Assess and feel if you have shifted into an energetic level, it is a subtle shift not a big drama or big bang.

5. When the Records are open, scan your body, mind, heart, spirit, and surroundings. Tune into your inner being with simple words and clarity. This step assures that you know how you are doing in all aspects of your being so you can transcend any emotions and mental thoughts that are not serving your highest good.(ie. Note the presence of body tension, mind confusion, perhaps heart broken, spirit sad, and per chance, the presence of other beings in the room, maybe spiritual guides.)

6. Ask questions regarding your patterns or blockages from your Akashic Records. Write the messages that you are receiving. Don't resist, judge or fear what is given.

7. These messages are for you to feel and listen. Allow this energy to flow in your body, mind, heart, soul and spirit.

8. Take notes and insights that you are receiving and ask how to clear if you need healing or releasing.

9. Be present, release and allow yourself to integrate.

10. It is very important to close your Records after consulting them. Thank the Ascended Masters, angels or spiritual guides for helping you. Thank the Lords of the

Akashic Records and close the Records. Say this "The Records are now closed, the Records are now closed, the Records are now closed. Be it done effortlessly, with ease, love and grace. And so it is."

Important note: You are not allowed to open your Akashic Records until the age of 18. Because your soul is still evolving and we do not want to interfere with your lessons.

Forgiveness and Release Prayer

This prayer is to declare to the Infinite Source, God or creator of All That Is that we are humbly asking for forgiveness for what our collective consciousness as sentient beings has collected and imprinted throughout the years.

Say this prayer however many times you want to throughout the day. Believe in miracles and this will heal your ancient lineage and those who have come in contact with you. You are a beacon of light. Shine your beautiful light to the world.

Prayer for Forgiveness:

"Infinite Source of All That Is, for myself, for all of my ancient lineage, for all of our relationships, for all sentient beings in all timelines, dimensions, space and realities, we are asking for forgiveness throughout our lifetimes."

In all our thoughts, words, emotions and deeds, for all those we have hurt, self and other, whether done consciously or unconsciously, we ask for forgiveness.

For all the times that we have created and experienced negativity, fear, pain, hatred, anger, gossips, abandonment, rejection, judgment, criticism, jealousy, lust, sloth, gluttony, envy, greed and wrath, we ask for forgiveness.

For all the times that we have created and experienced sexual rape, incest, abortion, infidelity, suicide and murder, we ask for forgiveness.

For all the times that we have created and experienced being unloved, unsafe, wounded, unsupported, for all times we did not trust, were not nurtured by our parents and others, we ask for forgiveness.

Infinite Source, we ask that we are all released, cleared and healed from all these energetic imprints in our souls and Akashic Records from all timelines, dimensions, space and realities.

We now ask that we be blessed with our new templates to create new patterns of positive and loving experiences. Infuse us with unconditional love, compassion, forgiveness, kindness, gentleness, liberation and freedom, truth, inner peace, joy, abundance in our lifetimes. Thank you, thank you, thank you, and so it is."

Suggested Deeper Questions:

When you are in the Akashic Records, you can ask deeper questions to gain more clarity. These are examples of questions that you can ask.

- What is happening in my body?
- What is my current emotional state?
- What is my soul's intention regarding this pattern of _____?

- How can I open my heart?

- Please go deeper and provide me more information

- Do I need to rephrase my questions differently?

- What is the root of this issue? How did I adopt this pattern?

- How can I clear this? How has this issue served those involved?

- What do I need to learn from this? (person/pattern/process)

- Am I ready to release this from my life?

- What is the new pattern that needs to replace the old?

- Is the contract complete?

- Am I holding any remnants of this issue in any of my other bodies? (mental, emotional, astral, etheric, etc)

- Where are they and how can I clear them?

- What steps do I need to take in order to create?

- What is the sacred contract?

- What is the mirror?

- What is the role? What is the gift? What is the lesson?

- Can I allow? Can I accept? Can I release?

- Can I be grateful?

- How can I speak the truth?

- How can I integrate this truth?

- How can I discern and check my integrity?

- How can I help myself move forward?

- How can I let go of my judgment?

- What are the archetypal patterns that I don't see?

- How can I let go of my control and my expectations?

- What is meaningful for me?

- What can I do to help myself?

- What are my blockages?

- What is blocking me from taking action?

- What are my fears?

- How can I undo these fears?

- How can I let go of these fears?

- How deep is my faith?

- Am I lying to myself?

- Am I allowing others to disrespect me?

Healing In The Akashic Fields

Our Family and the Akashic Contracts

The family that we are born to constitutes a big part of our Akashic Records. Our blueprints are intertwined with each member's souls purpose. We all have sacred contracts with each other that we are going to play major roles in our incarnation and lessons in life.

The conflicts and pain that are caused by our parents and siblings are part of our empowerment program in the future. We develop these entanglements with the members of our family to help us become empowered on our path. They are the catalyst for us to develop inner strength.

When we open our Records, we can see the bigger picture containing the lessons and purposes of each of our family members. It can be painful sometimes to forgive and let go. But this is a part of your soul's longing; to experience what true forgiveness means.

We are intricate parts of the whole. When we are able to see their participation in a bigger scheme of things, then we can know deep within that it was meant to be.

By going through the portal of forgiveness, we allow our soul freedom. Our load feels lighter. The blessings that we receive begin to pour out into our lifetime, without impediments. We can practice being grateful for the gifts that our family members have given us. Even though we have experienced negative situations, these are the catalysts of change.

Bless your family and shift your perceptions regarding past experiences. Transcend your victim consciousness and ascend for your highest good.

Begin an excellent practice of meditation, see each family member in your vision, send them love and forgiveness. Thank them for what they have given you. Bless any pain that you have felt with them and know everything has now come into a full circle of life.

Healing Family Karma

Healing the family's karma clears away those energetic imprints, attachments and bondage that are attached to our soul. We are unconscious human beings, who may keep repeating the same cycles all over again and again and again.

By experiencing the pain and sufferings of our family's karma, we rehash what we felt as children. When we grew up, our inner child archetype carried these lower vibratory frequencies in our energetic fields. As adults, we recreate the same emotions of fear or any blockage that we had experienced as a child. The same situations repeat in different forms of conflict. We immerse ourselves in chaotic patterns that are not healthy for us. We become unconscious creators of these conditions and habits. We need to become conscious of what is appearing in our realities in the current lifetime. Only then can we connect these emotions and piece them together to transmute our patterns. The clarity that ensues from this process of understanding infuses love and light within.

In our ascension process, we are literally being called to detach from the lower vibrations of our emotions. These lower vibrations are the varied forms of anger, sadness, worry, fear, shame, guilt, pride, grief and apathy. There are emotional signatures that our family's karma is carrying, passed on through each generation. It forms addictions, attachments and bondage in our energy fields and they are not healthy for us.

Any emotions that make us feel small, restricted, contracted or restrained are not serving our highest good. These energetic imprints, like entities, are alive, sucking our light out and creating shadows in our energy fields, creating heavy clouds within our psyche and aura. During the process of detachment or releasing these emotions, we will attract situations that will mirror our past pain in our lifetime. It is not an easy space to be in because we are challenged once again to face our hidden conflicts with other members of our family.

Our parents, like octopuses extend their tentacles as their children. When the children are co-dependent with their parents, they are insecure of themselves. They need to nurture their souls and in order to do this they attach to their parents in unhealthy ways. Their souls feel fragmented and in a twisted way creating this co-dependency with their parents. Observe how you are relating with your parent and if it is a destructive pattern. Reflect and investigate how you are using your parents, if it's an attachment for your insecurities.

Healing karma starts from knowing the emotional signatures that are bonding you with your family. Acknowledge the patterns, conditions and cycles. When did this pattern start in your life? At what age did you duplicate this pattern? When do you feel some stuck or heavy energy in your body? What is the main emotion that is tied to this pattern? What is your coping mechanism?

Families have their own roots of bondage. These are the emotions that were expressed and unconsciously collected in the gene pool of our bloodline. The DNA and RNA have these imprints in our collective unconscious. Our family's history is written in our Akashic Records. We need to understand these entanglements in order for us to transcend these lower vibrations of our consciousness.

Murder or suicide in the family can intensify suffering from pain, anger, revenge, resentment, rejection, abandonment, betrayal and many other emotions that are not healthy for us. We are here to transcend this experience. We are the karmic healers. We are the light bearers of our lineage. We clear the path for our generations to come with love and light. It is an important process of clearing our karma with our ancestors.

The Masters of Light will help us attain our soul healing when we open our Akashic Records to review, see, and know what patterns are kept within our heritage. The gatekeepers guide us in our ascension process to help us accelerate our growth towards wholeness. We then see the bigger picture of our lives. Free will is always ours. We now choose and learn from our lessons. When we understand, we become more aware, awake and enlightened about the effect of our thoughts, words, emotions, intentions and actions. We realize that all of these have bearing on our written Records. We become responsible for all of our conscious choices. Destiny is in our hands and we are governed by universal laws.

Steps to heal the karmic bondage in our family:

1. Open your Akashic Records. You can do this by yourself or go for a consultation.

2. When you open your book of life. Go into your heart space and forgive yourself and others who have hurt you in this lifetime. State this: "I forgive myself for hurting others and I forgive others for hurting me consciously or unconsciously in all timelines, dimensions, space and reality. And so it is." Envision these people and feel the patterns that are being revealed to you. Heavy emotions vibrate in a lower frequency like resentment, judgment, anger, abandonment, rejection, and many others. These are the patterns of your karma, toxic to your life. As you probe

further, you can also have visions of other past lives you have lived. Remember the feelings that were triggered. They are the messages that are being revealed to you by the gate keepers.

3. Now it is time to release. Ask St. Germain and the Violet Flame to assist you. "St. Germain and the Violet Flame, please transmute all these energies that are not of light, name them: _____. I ask that these energies go back to the Source of love and light. Please infuse the void with unconditional love, forgiveness, compassion, kindness, abundance, inner peace, joy and bliss. (Add anything that you would love to bring into your life) Thank you, thank you, thank you. And so it is."

4. Close the Akashic Records. Thank the Lords of the Akashic Records for allowing you to have a glimpse of your Records. Now, close your book of life. It is very important to close your Records. "The Records are now closed, the Records are now closed, the Records are now closed."

As you learn and acknowledge the karmic bond that you inherited from your family, it is time to heal them in your Akashic Records. This is a multi-dimensional healing tool. All layers of your mental, emotional, etheric and astral bodies become clear in your book of life. We are releasing these patterns in all timelines, dimensions, space and reality. Ask the Ascended Masters to clear these and heal. Ask these energies to go back to the Source of love and light. When we clear some energies, we need to ask the Masters of Light to infuse love, peace, grace or any blessings that you would love to have.

Prayer:

We ask the Lords of the Akashic Records to open my book of life and allow access to my own Records. My name is _____(state your legal name) The Records are now open. (Repeat three times) I ask that my family's karmic bondage and energetic imprints in my book of life be cleared, released and healed. We ask these energies to go back to the Source of love and light. We ask the Archangels and angels to infuse the healing light and essence within my cellular level of memories, consciousness and existence. Thank you, thank you and thank you for this healing. My Akashic Records are now closed, they are now closed, and now closed. And so it is.

Healing Past Lives

How does reviewing past lives help us transcend our defeating patterns? Opening our Akashic Records can reveal to us our past lives. It can help us understand why we keep repeating the same cycles. It is so amazing how a past life can be a bridge for our wisdom to know why we keep repeating cycles and patterns that are not serving our highest good. When we understand the genesis of the issue, going back in time to a specific civilization, our soul can comprehend the roots of our behavior. We can modify our perceptions. And be lighter whilst understanding what is happening within us.

It is a challenge for us to tap into past lives when belief or religion sets limitation about reincarnation. Someone has to be truly open to delve into these mysteries of life. As we explore the Akashic Records, we find that our soul's journey becomes more expansive and boundless. Our souls have no concept of time and space, it is an infinite spark from the Source of all creations. The information, knowledge, and wisdom that we acquire and receive are beyond what our mind can conceive. It is crucial that we have an open mind and heart when we open our book of life.

Steps to Access Your Past Lives in the Akashic Records:

1. Before you open your Akashic Records, list the things in which you would like more clarity, especially

The cycles and patterns that you create that do not serve your highest good. I.e. addiction, suicidal thoughts, low self-esteem, etc.

2. Create a safe and sacred space with Archangel Michael and the Blue Ray. Light a candle and meditate.

Invoke your spiritual guides and Masters of Light. Ask your guides to help you open your Third Eye

Chakra to receive a clear inner eye vision of your past life. Surround yourself with high frequency vibrations of Apophyllite and Lapis Lazuli. They aid in stimulating and intensifying your inner vision as you receive the gift of clairvoyance.

3. Open the Akashic Records by saying, "Lords of the Akashic Records, gatekeepers, and the Lords of Karma, please open my book of life. My name is _____(your full legal current name), create a safe and sacred space for my highest good and healing. The Records are now open." Say this three times.

4. Your Records are now open and you can start asking your guides to reveal to you a past life that will help you understand why you keep repeating this pattern. Be specific about the pattern for example, "I am not intimate with my partner and I want to know our past lives together." Close your eyes, and see the vision that will be given to your inner eye. A vision of you together as monks in the Himalayan Mountains travelling together is a clear indication that you and your partner were

monks in the past. Feel the energy around this past life and feel the emotions around this particular timeline. You are tuning into this frequency of your soul during this past life. As you become more aware, you can ask quietly questions to go deeper and reveal more information. When you get that "aha" moment you can slowly open your eyes. You will find that the answer is so precise and clear. This will release your doubt and clear the karma between you and the other person. It becomes a bridge to cross that benchmark in your quest for answers. Your relationship will change for the highest good of all. Transformations will occur.

5. It is very important to close your Akashic Records after consultation, thank the guides, your gatekeepers and the Lords of the Akashic Records for giving you access and a glimpse of your past life. Feel the energy of healing from your Records. Now ask the Lords to close the Records, "The Records are now closed." three times.

Past Lives in the Akashic Records

When we are in the Records, we access the past life in this incarnation and other timelines. It is very interesting that we have the tools to change the past. This is because in the Akashic Records there is no time and space. We are all interconnected in all parallel lives. Whatever is happening now is interactive with our past as well. If we are experiencing blockages in the current lifetime, then we have carried the energetic imprint of that past life.

When we open our Records, and tap into the past that is blocking our highest potential, we are given a glimpse of the past that is affecting our stagnant energy. By going deeply within, we are able to transmute the energies of the past and release these from our energy fields. What we are changing is the vibration of the past, including our perceptions and beliefs embedded in that time and space. This healing will bring in the new patterns of awareness within our cellular level of memories and consciousness.

With the assistance of our Masters and guides we are able to elevate and transmute these energetic imprints. For example, if in our past life we lived as a monk, we may have carried the vow of poverty. In this timeline however, we are not monks anymore and we need money to live abundantly in our current lifetime. We need to go back to that timeline as monks and release these vows that we had taken from the past life. Consciously, we will be aware of these imprints in our contracts and will ask for help from our Masters and guides to release the burden of this scarcity and of our unconscious beliefs regarding money.

As we become conscious, we shift our perceptions and develop our self-esteem. We deem that we have the birthright to prosperity. This is a huge leap of our faith and consciousness. Living new patterns of thinking in our sub-conscious mind helps us in the development of new habits. The powers of healing past lives is an amazing tool for healing the current patterns that are appearing in this lifetime.

Healing from the Womb

When mothers are pregnant, they carry our emotional intelligence, consciousness and cellular memories. Depending on their holistic emotional and mental state of condition, we develop our emotional intelligence. The challenges arise when one aspect of our mother's emotional or mental state in the conception stage is imbalanced or unwholesome, then these flaws are hidden or lay dormant in our biology and energy fields. When these emotions are triggered and activated within our cellular memories and consciousness, we reenact these lower emotional frequencies such as anxiety attacks, panic or anger. These layers of unconscious memories will rise up in our biological system manifesting as illness or "dis-ease" signaling to us where our wires are crossed. When we are experiencing stress or pain, it is our body talking to us; it reveals where our energy is leaking or not in alignment.

Most of us focus our attention on the pain and never really listen to our body's message. Our body receives and transmits information every nano-second of our existence. When we become still, the messages relay. We have to ask our body parts: why is the pain happening and how we can relieve it? It is deeper than we think, layers upon layers of emotional and mental chromosomes have been passed on from generation to generation, through all past lives in all timelines, dimensions and realities. We are healing all these in our conscious awareness when we tap into our Akashic Records. We are given a window of opportunity to see what is blocking us from being wholesome and relieved from all of these sufferings in our bodies and timelines that we are living in.

When our relationships with our mothers are not healed, it is difficult to connect to our divine feminine energy because of the misaligned energies between our mothers and ourselves. In order to heal this, we have to first forgive our mothers for whatever things or mistakes they have caused us. Then, we forgive ourselves for harming our mothers. This congruency with our souls is about light and love; it helps us transcend this lifetime and release the baggage that we are carrying energetically. The healing connects our souls in eternal timelines and realities. We become secure with our existence on this planet Earth and our roots are grounded deeper within our consciousness. We feel that we belong and are loved.

This is a powerful mantra or prayer in releasing and clearing blockages or any illness in our energy fields.

"I release and clear my mother's energy cords and fields, blockages, unconscious negative beliefs, attachments, entities, beings, and souls that are in my energy fields from all timelines, dimensions and realities to go back to the source of love and light."

Anytime we are releasing or clearing, remember to fill the void or gap with a positive affirmation or prayer, bringing in love and light to the space. "I now ask for the blessings of healing of my mother's womb, love, light, abundance, joy, peace and freedom to receive these from the Divine providence of the source of everything, to fully manifest these gifts in my timeline right here right now, Amen."

Healing Pain from Abortion, Miscarriages and Stillbirths

The painful experiences of mothers who have lost their children due to abortions, miscarriages or stillbirths, creates an emotional, energetic imprint in the womb. There is an energetic cord attached to the traumatic event and it creates an emotional pain body inside the wombs of women. The Sacral Chakra Energy Center becomes blocked and it creates suffering in our relationships and sexuality. The feminine goddess energy is misaligned with the soul's purpose.

When conception happens, the DNA of a man and woman becomes one, creating a living conscious soul. This fetus grows for approximately 9 months in the womb and absorbs information from both gender's blueprints. We are looking at the Akashic Records or the soul's imprints of these people and how it affects the life of this soul inside the womb. We call this soul genetic encoding, not only about biological function but also in our soul level encoding of our ancient bloodlines, DNA and energetic imprints of our family's ancestors.

The history of our human evolution affects us in our existence. All that was created and imprinted here in mother Earth is a part of our collective consciousness. Therefore, we live in the quantum soup of all that is. When we are unconscious of our creations, we create sufferings in our lives. We need to understand the soul codes of humanity in order to process our human conditioning.

When mothers lose their children in any form or way, they create an emotional painful body in their Sacral Chakra. This energy center resides in the reproductive center of human beings. It is a vortex or wheel of energy that connects us to the power of sex, money, creativity and relationships. We create a blockage of never ending cycles of events that result in painful situations. This happens when we don't heal our pain from this energy center. Unconsciously, we recreate fear and other lower emotional signatures of pain.

The mothers need to clear and heal their issues, find a soul healer to help transcend their pain. Because of the deeper wounds that this pain carries, it is necessary that a soul or spiritual healer is consulted. When the mothers' wombs are not healed, the children that inherit these emotional signatures of pain will recreate situations in their lifetime like a cycle of karma. This is the karmic bond between parents and children. You can identify these painful emotional signatures that play within your family dynamics such as anger, guilt, abandonment, fear, shame, anxiety and many other emotions that are toxic to our spirit.

It is important that mothers' wombs be healed to create children that are carrying the light consciousness of love. To evolve we need to transcend these sufferings. We don't need to stay in the dark or go through painful events. We can help others transform by sharing light and love. We are always being guided by our Higher Selves, our Souls. We are being assisted by our Ascended Masters, Archangels, angels, Beings of love and light, and our loved ones from other dimensions. We need to consciously call them to create a safe and sacred space around us. These beings of Light transmute our blockages and transmit new encodings of light into our DNA to fully ascend this lifetime.

We have been in the dark for eons of time. This is the new horizon of healing for our consciousness and the species. In order to hold the sacred space for mother Earth Gaia to fully ascend with our existence, we are asked to carry these light codes of our souls into full alignment with her gala. The high vibrations of our humanity will help our species to evolve into light beings of love. We cannot allow sufferings to bring us down. We transcend these dark nights of our soul into treasures in the light. When you are experiencing darkness you have the power to call in light. The light penetrates each and every particle of our souls.

Call the masters to your situations; this allows healing in your family lineage. Cut the cords of attachments, stories of pain, blockages, fear, unconscious negative beliefs, human conditioning, entities, negative emotional signatures and patterns. **St. Germain and the Violet flame** together with **Archangel Zadkiel** work great in this department. Invoke them and light a candle, create a sacred space. Heal the children of our future. Bring the light and love and we will ascend in these lifetimes and create a magnificent experience.

May you find light in times of darkness, comfort in times of sorrows, inner peace in times of chaos, understanding in times of confusion, forgiveness in times of guilt, surrender in times of grief, and eternal love from your beloved children. They never really left; they remain always a part of you inside your precious hearts and divine souls. Eternal souls we are.

Healing Relationships

Relationships are contracts that you had agreements with in your Records. However, when that relationship ends, it does not really matter if the experience was negative or positive. The contracts of your souls meeting together and experiencing life, was predestined in your Records. You have agreed to meet up again in this lifetime and fulfill someone's lesson. When we are aware of our Records and ask questions about the lessons that we are learning from the other person, we become more conscious about our relationships. We see the bigger picture of why we are together and thus create harmony and peace. We gain deeper understanding about our soul's mission here on earth.

When a couple goes for a healing, this can create a bridge for their relationship to thrive. They release the pattern of blame and judgment. They become more forgiving and truly understand why they are together. Sometimes a person can come for healing and advice on what they are to do with their relationship. They get clarity and perhaps, the power to cut the cords between their contracts that are not serving their highest good. The eye of the soul reflects what they are seeking for answers. Deep within, a spark of understanding and truth ignites the internal fire. This healing session from their Akashic Records can catalyze the shift that they needed.

The soul remembers the purpose they came here to fulfill. Consequently, they release their dependency on the other person. Clearing contracts, vows and agreements in your Akashic Records is a powerful tool to finally let go of the other party. I witnessed huge transformations with couples who came for healing. They regained freedom to express what they want in life. Suddenly, it made sense rather than just living without a sense of self-recognition and self-esteem.

The record's energetic imprint empowers and creates a safe space for each one of us to feel and heal the wounded self. We can become aware of our soul's participation in our creations. We become responsible and accountable for our actions and thoughts. Our soul's journey goes deeper into Self and how we react with those we care about. It is now easier to let go of attachments, and not being able to forgive. We can reach the point of forgiveness of ourselves and of all others in all lifetimes.

We truly do not know when we hurt others in other timelines and dimensions. So, we go through life holding this bittersweet love between others. The beauty of opening your Records is that it allows us to go through the forgiveness portal, where we forgive ourselves and forgive others for any harm that we have done consciously and unconsciously. We can never know truly what we did to these people in our past lives. Opening the Akashic Records energetically clears the path for us to live lighter and more lovingly.

Relationships can be confusing when we are going through chaotic times. We forget that misunderstandings can come from old contracts that all parties signed up for. For example, if the two of you had contracts to become monks, you will find that there are times that you want to be alone on your own.

This can trigger separation and anxiety. In order to understand these emotions that are arising, you may see your contract and vow as a monk upon opening the Records. You may then understand that these are triggers from a past life. Now, that both of you have chosen to live together in this lifetime, each one of you can understand that being alone is fine and does not mean that you are going to be separated.

Giving permission to allow independence for both parties will help ease the separation anxiety. There can be an energetic bond between two monks. We can clear this via our Akashic Records so that you feel more at home with the other person and feel open to receive love.

Clearing Entanglements

In our relationships, we can be in the midst of entanglements and not understand why. There are a lot of factors why we are together with a person and our family circle. These are our contracts and all of us can be entangled to the core of our emotional patterns, mental thoughts and past lives.

Entanglements can be deceiving, as we crave to belong. But when the core of a relationship is not healthy, we can feel at loss. How can we tell if the relationship is entangled? By our emotions, we have to be aware of these signs and reflect on what is lying beyond the surface.

Recognize that there is something off when we get stuck in the midst of chaos. This is a sign that there is power control or struggle. What is this situation calling for? Boundaries and respect. The vibration of others is not for us to take. Do not pay attention or react to things that are not serving your highest good. We have the power to allow only the good things that serves us. We do not need the drama of others. We can create a force field around us with the Masters of Light that protects us against any attacks or draining of our energy. This will help us sustain our inner strength in the midst of chaos. We can send love and light to those concerned.

These entanglements can be seen in our Akashic Records and our work with the Masters of Light. They help us see the bigger picture.

Here is a list of things to do in these situations:

1. Ask our spiritual guides, "What are we learning from these contracts?"

2. Forgive others for the unconscious harm that they have done in all timelines and dimensions.

3. Forgive ourselves for hurting others unconsciously and consciously.

4. Ask Archangel Michael and the Blue Ray to cut any cords of attachments and entanglements with the people in our lifetime. Ask Archangel Michael to send these energies back, returning to the Source of love and light. Send love and light to those who are concerned.

5. Be aware of your participation, act responsibly, and know that there are spiritual guides that can help you heal these entanglements. Maintain peace within yourself and send that peace toward others.

Clearing Contracts, Vows and Agreements

Contracts, vows and agreements are recurring patterns that attract lower vibrational frequencies to our energy fields. They are restrictive, feeding on our fears and hindering us in our ascension process.

Signs and symptoms of blockages:

1. When you feel stuck with your career choices

2. Feeling constricted in a relationship

3. Having legal litigations or court hearings with another person

4. Unable to move forward with choices

5. Conflicts with others

6. Unable to manifest money

7. Unable to keep a relationship

8. Fear

9. Health conditions or illnesses

10. Accident prone

In this lifetime, we will find that we have existing contracts between souls seen or unseen that are not serving our highest good and it is time to release, heal and clear them in our Akashic Records.

Questions that can help someone know what, who, where and how you agreed to these contracts in these lifetimes, other timelines, dimensions and alternate realities:

1. Are there any contracts in other past lives with this person?

2. What types of contracts are there?

3. What is going on in my lifetime right now that is not working?

4. What are the patterns in this contract?

5. What did I agree to?

6. How am I using this contract in this timeline?

7. What am I getting from this contract?

8. What is my lesson?

9. Did I take a vow of celibacy, poverty and silence?

10. Am I ready to let go and release these contracts from my Akashic Records?

Now that you have identified the contracts that you want to release from your Akashic Records, it's time to open and work with the Masters of Love and Light.

As we open our Crown Chakra energy center, right at the top of our heads, we connect and receive this universal and cosmic golden light from the Akashic fields. Connect to the core column of light that sits in front of our spine, feel the expansion of our heart space and allow the opening of our hearts to the Akashic Records.

We call forth the Ascended Masters, Archangels and angels, Saints, Benevolent beings of Light, our Higher Selves, spiritual teams and guides and loved ones from other dimensions to protect us with white light and create a safe and sacred space for our healing and highest good.

We ask the Lords of the Akashic Records to open our Records, grant us healing, compassion, love, information, knowledge, messages and wisdom for our highest truth.

We thank all the Benevolent Masters of Love and Light that have come to assist us in our healing, the Records are now open, the Records are now open, the Records are now open. And so it is.

Meditation:

Visualize a door opening. Open the door that leads to your Akashic Records. See the library hallway and walk, looking around your surroundings. Feel the vibrations of the books surrounded with golden light. As you walk into this hallway, you will find a stand in front of you. Pick a book from the shelf and placed it on top of the stand. Open this book of your life and see the golden light coming out of this book. These are your Akashic Records. Now you are ready to see a vision or symbol from your Records that will help you remember your contracts.

You can start asking the questions about your contracts. Follow up with healing, releasing and clearing these contracts from your Akashic Records with the Masters of Light and Love.

Healing:

We ask **Archangel Michael** and the Blue Ray to come and cut any cords of attachments, energetic imprints, entities, souls, hooks or drains that are attached to these contracts pertaining to _____ name of person.

We ask **Archangel Gabriel** and the White Ray to release, clear and delete these files from my Akashic Records and create new contracts of empowerment, courage and truth.

Known and unknown, seen or unseen, all timelines, dimensions and realities, all alternate and parallel universes and galaxies, all sources and void.

By the power of grace, I now declare these contracts, vows and agreements to be released, cleared and healed. I ask the Lords of the Akashic Records to delete these files and clear all cellular levels of memories and consciousness. I release and heal gently with flow of ease, love and grace. And so it is.

Forgiveness prayer:

I forgive myself and others for hurting each other consciously and unconsciously, for these contracts that I have made in all timelines, dimensions and realities." Close your eyes and feel this in your heart space. Visualize these people that you have hurt, send them forgiveness, love and light. Release and breathe.

Closing prayer:

"We thank our Ascended Masters, Archangels and angels, Saints, Benevolent beings of Love and Light, our Higher Selves, spiritual teams and guides and loved ones from other dimensions.

We thank the Lords of the Akashic Records for allowing us access of our Records and for the healing, blessings, gifts of wisdom, information, messages and clearing of our contracts, vows and agreements. We ask this healing to be sealed with the sacred geometrical form of Merkabah to flow with ease, love and grace. Thank you, thank you and thank you. The Records are now closed, the Records are now closed and the Records are now closed. And so it is."

Cutting the Cords of Attachments

Throughout the evolution of humanity, we've carried energetic imprints from our ancestors, bloodlines, DNA, collective consciousness of our species, other timelines, dimensions and realities that we lived. Imagine all of these energetic imprints in the one vast expansive soul that we are, inside this physical body, we are definitely one complicated sentient being of Light living in the universal energy of light and shadows.

We create entanglements with all of these energies in our soul's vibrations because there is no time and space in this soul or light continuum. As we live here on Earth, we are simultaneously living in other dimensions that we can tap into. Unconsciously, we exist in other timelines of our expansive selves. We are tapping into the universal energy of light coming from all creations of the Source of all that is.

As we evolve we need to understand that like magnets, we need negative and positive ions to attract the full manifestation of our true self. As the Law of Attraction creates what we are inside, we become aware of what we have in our external physical reality. With that said, imagine your soul needs shadows to create a fulfilled blueprint in this third dimension. The light and shadow aspects of our existence will bring into fruition what our soul's blueprint entails. The wisdom is to know that we need to embrace our shadows to fully understand what we need to know about our true soul's purpose and grand design. Like a blueprint, we have a grand design from the Creator and our goal here is to manifest this in our reality. There are Laws in the Universe and one of these is the Law of Vibrations. When you become aware of the signature of your own vibrations, you become conscious of all your creations.

We live in a paradoxical world. What we think we see is not what it is truly intended for. Everything is a mirror of our own selves. If you are seeing the shadow of another person it is because you are putting attention to the shadow of this soul. This means something deeper within you is a shadow that needs light.

Pay attention to your thoughts and emotions, ask yourself these questions: "Where is this shadow coming from? What do I need to learn from this mirror? What is my lesson? How can I see this person in his highest light? What is it in me that needs light?" These questions will bring you into alignment with your Higher Self and your soul's perspective. The person that triggers you is the catalyst for you to move towards light.

Seeing the other person in shadow will teach us compassion and forgiveness, to be kind and gentle with ourselves and others. We need to know that we are all one in this unified consciousness. When we come from this perspective, we connect to the Divine essence. We become more sensitive to our needs and begin to pay attention to what is truly happening in our relationships with others. It is not an easy road that we tread, but the choice is ours. It is the light that penetrates our core being. It is the love that abides in our hearts that will direct us in our chosen paths.

We are empowered beings of light that hold this humanity. We cannot do it alone, we need the assistance of the Masters of Light. They are here to guide, direct and help us become wholesome beings of Light. We can become light showers to others when we have this radiance of light that illuminates all shadows.

We are being assisted by Ascended Masters, Benevolent Beings of Light, Archangels and angels. We are never alone. We belong to this universal light energy. We are one. Let us embrace our shadows and light, together we can make this an illuminated universe. We can create and grow beyond our imagination. We are powerful beings of Light and love. We are guided and always directed. Let us now face our conscious choices and be light and love for ourselves and others.

We cut cords and attachments by asking guidance and assistance from these Masters of Light. Ask **Ascended Master El Morya** and **Archangel Michael** with the Blue Ray**,** the leader of Archangels, to arm us with his protection and to cut the cords, attachments and entanglements in all levels of our consciousness, cellular memories, energetic fields, holographic matrices, bio-etheric fields, crystalline fields and all realities. Go into your Akashic Records and go back to the timeline when it was created and heal.

Ask **Archangel Metatron** to rewrite your Records, to bring all negative energies back to the Source of love and light. We ask these intentions for our healing, to gain clarity, direction, wisdom and knowledge on how we can align ourselves with our grand design. We are grateful to all of our Masters of Light that continually assist us in our ascension process.

Akashic Contracts

The Akashic contracts are people we connect with in this lifetime. Our paths cross and it makes a shift in our life. These contracts can be negative. They are tumultuous relationships. They are our triggers in victim consciousness. They are here, however, to empower us and assist us in transcending our consciousness. We can either change our perceptions to become a better person, or we can turn to lower vibratory frequencies, emotions like anger and non-forgiveness.

These contracts are here, in our blueprints, because we agreed to incarnate and meet each other in order to experience and learn our lessons. It is quite paradoxical in a sense, because the shadows that are created in our relationships actually direct us towards the light and that is what we come here to learn. For example, if your parents had abandoned you when you were a child, unconsciously in your contract, you were supposed to learn self-reliance and independence. In a positive light, you may in turn, support orphans and abandoned children because deep within you is a core of abandonment.

On the other hand, unconsciously you can be repeating the same pattern of abandonment with your own family, recreating fear until you get the lesson. We come here to experience the paradoxical meaning of life. When we truly experience ascension, we transcend our shadows and can be at one with all that is. The veils lift, and the light begins to dominate perception, we are able to forgive others and send blessings to those who are still in the dark.

How can we transcend these shadows? The secret lies within our self, when we know that we are the alchemist, we can shift any lead into gold.

Steps in shifting shadows into light:

1. Create a safe and sacred space. Reflect, meditate and journal with the shadow or negative situation.

2. Open your Akashic Records and ask," Lords of the Akashic Records please open my Records and state your full current legal name _____. The Records are now open, the Records are now open and the Records are now open. What is my Akashic contract with this situation and person?"

3. What is my lesson?

4. How can I release or heal this?

5. Am I ready to let go?

6. Ask the Masters of Light to come into your presence. Ask St. Germaine and the Violet Flame to transmute the negative energy, to release, clear and send these energies back into the Source of all that is.

7. Call Archangel Michael and the Blue Ray to cut any cords or attachments with the people concerned.

8. Call Archangel Raphael and the green Ray for healing.

9. Say the forgiveness prayer. "I forgive myself for hurting others consciously or unconsciously in all timelines, dimensions, space and reality. I forgive others for hurting me consciously or unconsciously in all timelines, dimensions, space and

reality. Envision these people that have hurt you and that you had hurt. Send them love and light."

10. Close your Records by acknowledging the Lords of the Akashic Records. "Thank you, thank you, thank you. Lords of the Akashic Records and Archangel Metatron, thank you for helping me heal. I now ask to close my records. The Records are now closed, the Records are now closed and the Records are now closed."

Current Lifetime Interacts with the Akashic Records

The Akashic Records or your book of life is interacting with what is happening in your life right now. It comprises of all your soul's vibrations which is a vast compilation of all your thoughts, intuitions, memories, visions, past lives, karma, words, emotions, relationships, contracts, vows, agreements, actions, conscience, society, environment, your DNA, RNA, which is the primordial substance of your soul when it leaves the Source and extends to its journey right now here in this incarnation.

It may be difficult to conceive but to make it simple, envision a book with chapters. The chapters are your journeys and experiences. When you open your book randomly, it opens to the chapter that you need to see. This glimpse into your Records will help you recognize what is happening in your current situation and how it is related to that chapter of your Akashic Records. It is important to have an intention and prepared questions before you come to consult your Records in order to have precise answers to what you are asking.

The gatekeepers will help you access your Records when you know the sacred prayer and portal to this path. Because we are complex and complicated multi-dimensional beings of light, there is a lot of information and messages available in your own Records. It is therefore easier to receive the message when we have the right questions to ask. What is given to us corresponds only to what we can handle at the moment. The more progress we make, the more we become accustomed to the ways we are receiving the information.

The information is relayed to you by your spiritual guides, which are closer to you in this incarnation. The higher you are in your vibrations the easier it is for you to access the higher beings or Masters of Light. As an example of how your current lifetime is affected by your Records, you may have difficulty in receiving abundance or financial gain in this lifetime. When we open your Records, there are energetic imprints of being a monk in your past lives. You had taken a vow of poverty, silence and celibacy in that particular lifetime.

To release these imprints, your awareness will shift and you may realize consciously that you are now having a different reality and that you are no longer a monk.

The healing takes place with the Masters that we are calling upon and who assist you in transmuting these blockages. Because your Records are open, it updates the information and upgrades what your soul's vibrations are receiving right now.

There is a seal of grace that is imprinted on the pages that were opened. I see this vision as the Masters placing a stamp on your scrolls and that means that the lesson was learned and you can now move forward to your new chapters of life without the blockage. It was quite an amazing experience for me to see this wonderful vision given to me as a healer.

Healing The Collective

Chaos in our Collective Consciousness

Our collective unconscious has created chaos within our archetypal energies. We tap into the unconscious state of our ego or shadows when we are in chaos. I created this **acronym for Chaos, Conflicts Hidden Arising in Oneself upon Seeing the truth.** When we are in the process of knowing our true essence or ascension, these conflicts or challenges rise up in our realities because the Universe is clearing the way for our purification. This means that chaos is the result of disharmonious patterns that were imprinted in our morphic fields in the past, and are now arising because the soul is going through an awakening from the old paradigm.

When our mind is awakening, it brings forth things that block us. These may be grief, guilt, anger, un-forgiveness and many other lower emotional vibrations in our energy system. We cannot see these energies but we can feel them. Our emotional body holds these vibrations and creates density in our physical body. This can lead to physical illnesses. Stress lowers our immunity and we become weak and sick.

We can untangle these patterns of chaos when we acknowledge that there is something within us that magnetized this situation. We are in denial when we think the other person is the only one concerned. Our projection may view the other person as the cause of this trigger. When we acknowledge our participation, we emancipate our shadows. Every part of our shadows are a part of us. We are fragments of the macrocosm. One is a part of the whole.

Origins of Chaos:

- Fear of the unknown

- Insecurity

- Attachment to people, things and places

- Ego

- Fear of change

- Power and control

- Taking things personally

- Separation

Questions to find clarity:

- What is it in me that drew this situation?

- Where am I not clear about what I want?

- What is my attachment to the story?

- What is the cycle or pattern of my chaos?

- What is my role?

- What is the Archetype animated in this chaos?

- How can I clear this?

- Am I ready to let go?

- Did I learn my lesson?

- Can I forgive others or myself?

- Can I bless others for giving me these lessons?

- Can I be at peace?

Gratitude

Be grateful for the chaos and learn the lessons. Life is about experiencing triumph over challenges. We are powerful beyond our knowing. We are multi-dimensional beings of love and light. Our wholeness is created in being light. To be light is to see beyond the shadows that we are facing. The shadow is chaos that is like a window opening for us to see beyond this reality. We are expansive. Overcoming our challenges, we turn them into golden light penetrating our collective consciousness. Forgive those who trigger you. Believe that we can make a difference in our humanity's evolution of consciousness.

As humans we are here to learn lessons. When circumstances are being offered as conflicts, we have the tendency to see these seemingly difficulties as no way out situations. This is where the alchemy begins, when we can stop and reflect "What is really hiding behind the conflicts in certain situations?"

The Universe is an intelligence force field. Everything that we see is a reflection of our own perception. When our "eye" lenses are blurry, we cannot see beyond the hardships. If we know deep within that this law of the universe exists, it is for us to be an observer of our creations. Therefore, we can be assured that what we experience in our energy field represents our inner thoughts, emotions and spirit. It is not an easy task to wrap our heads around this and say that everything is our creation. It takes a soul's perspective and wisdom to comprehend this equation regarding our creations. We see others as separated from us. When we are in the field of separation, our aim is to reach a state of oneness, our unified consciousness.

The Alchemy of Conflicts

It is an arduous process to be in a state of grace. Opening your mind and heart to allow for expansion will bring you new insight into the conflicts presented. What are conflicts?

Energetically speaking, they are an incongruence of frequency between individuals; individuals attempting to maintain a resonance of peace, harmony and love. The root of conflict is fear. Fear presents itself with walls of separation. It can manifest as anger, blame, judgment and rejection. In the true essence, both parties are expressing their lower vibratory frequency. This lower vibration results in unwanted behavior and attitude.

When we take responsibility for our creations of conflict, we can be in a space of resolution. This becomes an opening for the expression of our truth. Opening your heart and soul will reveal the deeper pain you may feel about the other person. This puts us in a space of vulnerability and it takes courage to attempt this. When pride stops you from being humble enough to take this stance, the process will take more time and it sometimes delays the healing for both parties.

What are the steps in shifting conflicts to harmonious relationships?

1. When conflicts arise, stop and reflect. Take responsibility for your participation in creating this between the two of you. You are the magnet of your situation.

2. Be humble and ask for an opening of your heart to find a solution to the problems. Ask for forgiveness of your actions and explain the truth coming from your heart. Let go of the ego.

3. Listen to the other person with an open mind and heart. Dig deeper and know that there are always roots and reasons for what has happened.

4. Find the emotional trigger and name it, for example, if the other person is making you feel that you are not good enough. Turn this around and own that your lesson is about "self-esteem". Our conflicts are our mirrors. Do not take it personally. It is simply a door opening for expansion to assist us in our ascension.

5. Know deep inside your heart that when a problem arises, it is an opportunity for you to utilize it. Then your negative reaction may shift into awareness. This awareness will bring you into a space of oneness.

6. Opening our mind and heart brings us into alignment with our truth. Know that we are powerful and we can shift everything with our clear perception coming from our heart.

7. The alchemy of conflicts in a nutshell is; take the conflict as positive opportunity for expansion and intimacy of the hearts. Be positive and know that you are always guided to go deeper into your soul level of expansion.

Healing the Fear of Intimacy

As a victim of sexual abuse, I find it difficult to be intimate with another person. In the past, I would delve into a series of relationships and found myself in the same cyclical patterns of brokenness. I knew the root of this was about my molestations as an infant. Later on in life, my father molested me sexually. I lost my trust in the people that I loved. As a consciously evolved person, I realized that healing sexual abuse takes a deeper multi-dimensional healing than any other abuse. Because our sexuality and spirituality is one, one sacred energy from which our Kundalini rises.

Kundalini is that flow of energy that is dormant within each of us. It lies in the base of the root of our spine and rises to the top of our head, to our Crown Chakra. When this is blocked due to trauma or abuse, our human consciousness can't reach the highest potential of awakening.

We need to activate this Kundalini so it can rise and flow energy within our system that fully attunes us to the universal energy field of the Cosmos. So it is important that we, as conscious evolved beings of light and love, awaken and become aware of our Kundalini. This will assist us in our Ascension process.

Accessing the **Akashic Records** helps me in my ascension process. It gives me a deeper understanding and clarity, why my soul chooses to experience darkness in this human consciousness. Akashic comes from the Sanskrit word "Akasha" meaning sky, ether or primordial substance before anything becomes a form. Just like an Architect would need to write a blueprint before building a house, the Akashic Records are the blueprints of our souls.

Everything is recorded in the Akashic fields, all our thoughts, emotions, words and actions. Can you imagine the vastness of it all? We have these immense living conscious libraries within our souls, where we can have access to find directions and revelations on how to release blockages and heal the wounds of our souls.

Each one of us has our own unique vibration of our souls Records. The Ascended Masters, Archangels and angels, our Higher Selves, spiritual teams, guides and loved ones from other dimensions assist us in our prayers to the Record Keepers to dispense to us grace and healing in our souls journeys. They are guarded and protected by the Lords of the Akashic Records. No one can have access to our Records without our permission or only when we learn how to access our own Records.

I ask my Record Keepers, what is my fear of having an intimate relationship? These are the blockages that came up. My intention in sharing this with you is that you may be able to find light in your own darkness and allow love to open your heart fully to breathe and just be. Creating room for healing and surrendering our fears and shadows, we trust that we are always loved and safe to belong with someone.

Blockages and Fear of Intimacy:

- Judgment of yourself and others

- Your story

- Yourself or ego

- The past

- Perfectionism

- No trust

- The need to be right

- Doubt

- Low self-worth and self esteem

- Fear of being hurt

- Unconscious negative belief of "I don't deserve to be happy."

- Unconscious negative belief of "I'm not good enough."

- Insecurity

- Unable to receive love

- Shame and guilt

- Closed heart, walls around the heart

- Vulnerability as a sign of weakness

How can I release these blockages and fears?

- Self-love, look into your eyes in the mirror every day and say "I am loved and I am beautiful."

- Open and allow communication to develop between you and the other person to grow

- Be aware of your negative thoughts about the other person and clear your mind

- Ground your thoughts into your heart and breathe

- You can't solve the problem with the same mind that created it, shift it to your heart consciousness

- Let go of fear, flow with the energy of love and surrender to the Divine source of love

- Trust your intuition and gut feelings

- Honor your worth, value yourself and respect your existence

- Remember you deserve the best of everything

- Ask **Archangel Chamuel** and the pink light to assist you in healing and clearing brokenness.

- Ask **Archangel Raphael** and the green light for healing the sexual trauma and injuries in your cellular level of memories and consciousness and create a new template of healing, compassion and kindness for yourself and others.

Healing Sexual Abuse

Healing a child's trauma regarding sexual abuse is a multi-dimensional task. We are multi-dimensional beings of light and love. The physical realities that we experience are quite difficult to understand, why did this happen to us? There are a lot of factors that we need to consider in healing these traumas to be fully healed.

The mental and psychological issues involve, emotional and pain body, astral or out of body disassociation, unconscious negative beliefs, fear of intimacy, soul and negative entities clearing, and parents broken relationships. These are heavy in our energy fields and overwhelming for a person to go through. We need to shine light on these shadows in order to help our human collective consciousness. We need to raise our vibrations in healing sexual abuse.

The mental and psychological factors involved can take a form of creating another persona or multiple personalities to protect their own vulnerable selves. A person who was hurt would invent a world where they are isolated or withdrawn from others. They develop an empathic body that can feel pain from others very easily but they may not be able to know how to shield themselves.

Relationships can trigger their underlying stress and can cause a nervous breakdown if not detected early. Counseling and bringing clarity to the trauma can help our mental functions and wholeness. The vulnerable child may feel unwanted, dirty, abandoned and needs help feeling safe and secure within themselves.

At the emotional and pain body, we attract the person we are with. When we are not healed, we magnetize a person who has the same vibrational frequency. Most sexually abused children attract others who are sexually abused as well. The wounds of the inner child will be exposed within the relationship. When we are unconscious of the existence of our pain body, we recreate the same situation over and over again. Until we become aware of the dysfunctions within our consciousness, only then do we shift into lighter ways of dealing and facing our shadows.

Out of body and astral projections are ways of escaping the pain of abuse. When we are experiencing abuse, our spirit finds a way out, out of pain. We can experience out of body and astral projections in order to be numb from the pain and suffering that we are currently feeling. It becomes a natural path of disassociation from our current situation.

We need to recognize a path to ground ourselves and face what is happening in our reality. Our spirit needs grounding into our manifested selves to fully function as whole. Our Higher Self has to align with our body to fully manifest our heart's desires and soul's purpose.

We may develop a lot of unconscious negative beliefs about ourselves when we are sexually abused. The image that we are not good enough, our body is not beautiful because we feel dirty inside may haunt us. There may be a separation belief that others are thinking negative things about us, leading to paranoia. Feelings that we are failures and miserable situations follow us. We become isolated because of these unconscious negative beliefs, patterns and conditioning that we develop throughout our adult lives. We have to know and shift these into our awareness to bring light into these shadows.

Fear of intimacy is very common with sexual victims. We run away from relationships so fast when the possibility of intimacy with another person arises. We may feel suffocated and that the relationship is not going right. We blame and project that the other person is not right for us. We feel bad for ourselves and guilty with hidden emotions behind all the dramas that we are presenting. We find ways of ending a relationship to justify our hidden fears. We are afraid to open our hearts and fully receive another soul into our being. We cannot experience intimate sharing because of our shadow, our past is too complicated and we feel that we are not entitled to be happy. We are different and we feel best left alone. These are the shadows of our unconscious thoughts.

Take note and handle one day at a time to raise and lift your spirit. Allow the light to penetrate your fear. Let the beautiful experience of loving another soul enter your being. Embrace your fear, allow and open your life to experience vulnerability, honesty and truth.

A major part of healing sexual abuse is Souls and Negative Entities Clearing. The portal of sexuality is sacred to our soul. When we make love, the spirit intertwines with the spirituality and energy fields of the other person including the spirits that are attached to their energetic field. We are energy, and entities or spirits may attach to us. This is why cleansing and clearing are essential in our daily lives.

Our Sacral Chakra energy is a sacred womb of creation. We connect to our Divine Source as co-creators of our existence using this portal. If it is not clear, we cannot manifest our heart's desires. We need to clear this chakra. The Shiva Lingam, a Holy stone from India, helps us cut the cords from all sexual encounters that we've had. We are also clearing past sexual cords from all timelines, dimensions and realities. The entities that linger attached to our energetic fields need to be cut off. We send them to the Light for transmutation into higher purpose and good.

Healing our Root Chakra involves healing relationships with our parents. We can't be grounded or supported by the universe if we are not rooted to the abundance of Mother Earth Gaia. The spirit of Gaia helps us feel supported, loved and secured in all ways. Healing takes forgiveness and total forgiveness includes forgiving our ancestral lineage and bloodline. We may find that most of the time in our family history, we are carrying these abuses throughout space and time. Our collective consciousness is asking us to heal this in our existence to help our future children have a bright and shining lighted soul's path in their journeys to Mother Earth.

May our experiences bring us more Light, Love and Joy to share with our evolution of consciousness, Beloved!

Hidden Shadows in Our Collective

We need to understand that our hidden shadows are here right now to help us clear our Souls. They are energetic imprints from our Akashic Records. These are patterns and experiences such as abuse as a child, behavior that has been passed on through ancestors, other people's judgments of us, lower vibrations of our emotions and thoughts such as anger, abandonment, jealousy, envy, shame, guilt, lust, craving, desire, separation, fear, our inability to receive love for oneself, not good enough, injustice, insecurity, worry, doubt, pain, scarcity, unable to trust, unable to love, and many more shadows that you can think of.

We are now blessed with the grace of the divine energy to wash away all these blockages from our energy system, holographic, crystalline, and bio-ethereal fields. Clear and release these energies that are not serving our highest good. We have the power to do so with the assistance of the Masters of Light. **Archangel Michael and the Blue Ray** is a powerful resource for cutting any cords of attachments from these toxins. **St. Germaine and the Violet Flame** is our Ascended Master that transmutes all energies that are not of light. We can ask the Archangels and angels to infuse us with their love, compassion, forgiveness, kindness and joy.

When we are calling for help, we surrender our situations. We are co-creators of everything that is in our fields. Whatever is on our plate, we are responsible for. With this reality, we can somehow gauge where we are and what we need to clear. When creating new templates, we have to recognize what blockages we have. Ask questions in your Akashic Records to receive the messages from the gatekeeper. You will be guided by your spiritual guides.

Cultivate your relationships with your spiritual guides. Like friendship, we need to spend time, energy, and communication to develop a strong intimate relationship with the Masters. These Masters of Light are the same, they want us to fully know them and how they can assist us in our daily lives. Listen to your intuition. When you feel that you are blocked in some areas, ask for clarity. Align your mind and your heart. Balance your feminine and masculine energies to fully receive and give love for yourself and others. Surround yourself with supportive and uplifting people. Let go of any expectations of the outcome. Be yourself at all times.

Know that these shadows are here to create a higher version of your Self. If you find you are triggered by others, forgive yourself and the people that have hurt you. The energetic cord is cut between you and others. Create a bubble of golden light around you at all times to create a filter or boundary for protection. The entanglements that are created when you are around others can bring in lower vibrations and make you feel sick when you are an Empath.

Knowing your shadows will help you in your ascension process. For example, you know that your triggers are judgment. When you were small, you received judgments from others that hurt you. You are still carrying these cords and hidden anger. You find yourself in a situation where you have judgmental eyes, meaning, it is easy for you to judge others without knowing them. This is a red flag about your shadow effect, it is a sign to dig deeper. Where did you experience being judged in the past? It can also be a past life, see a healer for this type of situation. When you ask the Masters of Light to clear these judgments in your Soul, right after that, ask them to fill in the void with love and light and any other qualities that you want to have like compassion, kindness, and peace.

Sacred Prayer:

"I ask my Ascended Masters, Archangels and angels, spiritual guides and teams, loved ones, my Higher Self, the gatekeeper and the Lords of the Akashic Records to clear, release all these energies and templates of lower vibrations namely _____ (name whatever it is that you want them to clear like: anger, judgment, abandonment, fear, scarcity) consciously and unconsciously in my Akashic Records, in all timelines, dimensions, space and reality. I also ask to fill the void with love, light, peace, joy, abundance, bliss, and miracles for my highest good and highest potential. May I serve my soul's purpose with pure awareness, humility, compassion, and kindness to all sentient beings. May I be of service towards our ascension and become a channel of grace, love, and light for the highest good of all. Thank you, thank you, and thank you. And so it is."

*Remember to close your Akashic Records every time you open them. The Records are now closed, the Records are now closed, and the Records are now closed.

Brokenness is the Bridge to Wholeness

We are all in a soup of the collective consciousness of humanity. It gives me a sense of security, knowing that we are all in the same boat. We all go through the same crises one way or another. Shadow and light perspectives encompass the spectrum of our lives. To be whole necessitates being broken first. How can we be in this state if we didn't know what brokenness means?

The beauty of being whole is the journey not the destination. We gain inner strength, courage and empowerment when we go through the stages of being broken into being whole. So don't fret when you find you are temporarily in the broken state. There is hope. Therefore, become an observer of your journey. This is the transitional state when we become aware of our conditioning and patterns. Repeating the same patterns and cycles of our shadows, expecting different result is insanity. Truly allowing ourselves to let go and be fully in the present moment, gives us a space to create a different pattern and to live a new life.

It is a soul's journey to experience shadows and yet be able to see the light. Our stories are being created as we live each and every moment of our lives. What kind of stories are you creating? Is it of miseries and defeat or victory and happiness? We are the co-creators of our lives with the Source. Our awareness is the key to this freedom and liberation from the illusions of ego.

The Ego would prefer to be small and attached to the world. But spirit is expansive, not confined or restricted.

Spirit has no limitation; it is boundless. We have this spirit to remind us of our truth. Our souls are whole not broken. Because of our ego, we forget our truth. The ego attaches us to this mindless way of thinking.

To think expansively, we need to embrace our ego and be appreciative of our existence. Ego is part of our incarnation. We want to incorporate that which makes us whole. Whatever exists is a part of one. All the aspects of our shadow and light is part of who we are. When we reject darkness, we will not be able to see the light. We are in this dichotomy of polar opposites. What we are, we attract. When we embrace our ego, we start to see the beauty of being whole and encompassing the polarities of life.

Our brokenness will pave the way to being whole. When we become aware of our own dramas and shadow, we attune to our light template. There is no right or wrong and no judgment for what we choose to experience in this lifetime. We are here to remember who we are and to return to our home.

Our victim consciousness is a part of our human journey. To transcend these experiences and become empowered is our transition. Instead of getting stuck in the lower vibrations, we raise our consciousness and vibrate in a higher frequency. Being broken helps us not. Rather, it holds us captive in the entrapment of our own illusions. The voices in our head are always there but awareness is the key to our awakening.

Let go of thoughts that create harm and surrender to the flow of life. Feel whole not broken. Let go of the stories of being wounded. You are now in the new energy of our collective universal consciousness. We are receiving these new templates of our new energies to be co- creators of our new consciousness. We cannot go back anymore, we are here to transcend these lifetimes and connect to our Higher Selves. Being whole is feeling content with our incarnation and fulfilled with what we create and can be.

How can we simplify being whole?

1. Be grounded. Nature keeps us grounded. Walk in nature. Communicate with nature's plants and animals. They vibrate in a high frequency.

2. Be authentic, speak from the heart and truth will set you free. Stay away from lofty ideas.

3. Be simple. Simplify things. Don't complicate things by staying inside your head. State what you want and know what you want.

4. Be focused and clear with what you want to create in your life. Follow your heart's desires.

5. Open your heart to receive and give love. Love is the most powerful force in the universe. Magnetize what you want to manifest.

6. Be honest with yourself, accept where you are and let go of things that do not work for you. Surrender to the flow. Do not resist things.

7. Stay away from drama. Do not make other people's stories yours. Set your boundaries.

8. Do not worry about things that are not here. It does not serve you any good. Know the problem and take it as a door of opportunity to expand your horizon. Be in the present moment.

9. Follow your intuition. Know your access to your Akashic Records. Consult your actions and trust your instincts. Your gut feelings are your guide to your lighted path.

10. Be happy and content for what you have. The relationships that you have are your blessings. They are your treasures in this lifetime. Be grateful and know that you are loved by the universe always.

Soul's Vibrational Frequency and Templates

One is all that is.

The Source is a reflection of all singular creations experiencing various multi-dimensional frequencies of light.

The Soul is an expansive vortex of universal energy that co-creates multi-dimensional templates that exist in infinitesimal beings of light and love. The Soul incarnates choosing templates to experience different levels of creation.

Freewill exists in this co-creation to establish harmony, unity and order in the universal laws. The Prime creator governs the universal laws. In order for souls to co-create light, they access power from the Source of all that is. The soul has choices. Shadows usually point out in which direction we choose to follow. When the soul chooses darkness, the light is temporarily dimmed down. When the soul recognizes that the shadow is a part of the illusion or ego, it will find the light that dissipates the shadows or fears.

Shadows are fears of our own light. When we are not aligned with our Higher Selves, we cannot find fulfillment in this incarnation. Powerful light has the codes to connect us to our Akashic Records. We stall or procrastinate to shine this bright light, afraid of being seen by others. When we start to see our own light, we then create unification of our light templates. We become the Master of our light. We unify and vibrate in the frequency of light. We become one with the Source of all that is. The light that we radiate helps others to see their own light. Thus, we are one light or souls reflecting to each other the light of the universe. We are the light of the multi-universes that we've been exploring through eons of time and space.

There is no time and space in this multi-dimensional state of being. When the veil is lifted, the hidden and unseen things are revealed to us in our Third Eye Chakra. By activating the pineal gland that holds the electro- magnetic fields of our existence, we become attuned to the synchronicity and harmonious movements of the universe. Past lives, present and future lives all exist in this universal energy. We are encoded with these memories and consciousness. It triggers our future lives when we are open to receiving the messages of the universe. Our radar detector is our physical body and our sensations.

We become blinded by our own ego and we doubt the messages that are being given to us. This is the time to open, attune and receive the language and symbols of the universe communicating to us through our physical bodies. The template of our physical body is designed to signal to us that which is happening inside our energetic fields. Forms or illness manifested in our realities are first created in the wiring of our energetic fields. These are the densest forms of our creation, Third dimension.

The way we think is totally the opposite of how the universe works. Take the opposite of how you think and function, this will show you the new template of our mental fields. We need clarity, direction and focus in our thoughts to co-create our highest potentials with the universal energy. Accepting our multi-dimensional state will help us in our creations and expressing our heart's desires. These mental thoughts need grounding to Earth's magnetic fields in order to infuse the light informational codes within our human biology systems. The information that is given to us can only manifest when grounded. Our neural pathways will not be able to take all the light codes that are being sent to us when we are not grounded to our Mother Earth. We could burn our wiring and our nervous system may not function in this accelerated pace of transformation.

It breeds fear when one is receiving too much information, ungrounded. We have to ground the thoughts that are affecting our vibrational state. To live in freedom, we need to detach ourselves from this material world. Free our spirit and we free our souls from shadows that trap us in our physical bodies. When we attain this freedom, our soul reaches the vibrational state of light and love. We connect with the information that the universe is giving us. It attunes us with our home and our light frequency increases in every cellular level of communication with the universal energy of light and information.

The mastery of our physical and mental templates gives us attunements to our soul's highest vibrational state which is love and light. What are the steps in attaining mastery of these templates? How can we maintain these high vibrational states of consciousness?

Are we ready to accept the responsibilities of living this high vibrational state of being? We are here to guide and assist in the raising of humanity's vibration to help accelerate our souls in ascension.

Steps in reaching our souls highest vibrational state of being Light and Love:

1. Awareness of our emotions, mental thoughts and physical bodies will attune us in our levels of Vibrations. Wisdom does not allow thoughts that will harm us. Let go of harming thoughts and be still.

2. Don't resist, what we resist persists. Listen to the signs and lessons in this present moment. What is the u universe telling you?

3. Open your heart and mind. Don't judge. Stay clear of what others think of you. You are unique and one of a kind. You are encoded with the universal creation and that makes you powerful.

4. Express your authentic self, be truthful and impeccable. Face your fears and infuse light into the s shadows of your creations.

5. Accept where you are. Don't judge yourself. Be gentle. Bestow kindness and compassion upon yourself and others.

6. Harmonize scattered thoughts. Unify and have inner peace.

7. Be grateful for all your blessings. Be of service to others.

8. Let go of attachments. Go with the flow.

9. Integrate all the aspects of your being, living multi- dimensionally.

10. Be present, happy and peaceful.

How to Manage Being an Empath?

An Empath is someone who is highly sensitive to their external forces, to things, to the emotions of others, to planetary movements, to the environment around them, to chemicals, perhaps to food, and to the pain and suffering of others.

When I was growing up, I remember feeling my family members' pain and conflicts. I would be affected by what is going on in their personal lives and I would try really hard to be the peacemaker of the family.

In the 23 years of my career as a nurse, I realized I needed to know how I could function in this environment without losing myself to it. How could I be centered and balanced and not be affected by the toxicity in my environment.

When I studied the Akashic Records, my senses and gifts were heightened and I had to go through the initiation process of knowing and learning how to manage the gift of being an Empath. Without these tools, I could not be in a space of healing and helping others in their awakening process towards ascension.

The boundaries that I needed, the sacred space that I had to make in order to shield myself from any energies, were crucial for my highest good. As an Empath, I needed to know my purpose and how I could filter myself from others, to center myself and to function in my environment.

We are light workers and because we are here to bring in Light for others to see their light within, others who are searching and seeking this light will be attracted to us. The shadows that they are in are just that, fear not realizing that they are love.

That is why when they encounter Empaths, they feel they can pour their heart out and trust that they can reveal whatever is bothering them. If we are not aware of who we are as Empaths, we will be carrying other people's pain and we may feel drained. We may not know or understand that we can actually have tools to use in order to be empowered and help others in their shifts. We can only help others when we master our own energies and vibrations. It is important to take care of Self first before attempting to help others in crisis.

Steps in managing being an Empath:

1. In meditation, ask your Ascended Masters, the angelic realms, your spiritual guides for protection before you leave the house. Send these Masters wherever you are going.

2. Be aware of your surroundings; scan your body, mind, heart, spirit, soul and other beings in the room.

3. Remember that you chose to vibrate in the high frequency of love and light. Stay focused and centered in your own sacred space.

4. When listening to other people's stories, be an observer. Do not take their stories as yours. Focus on your high vibrations. Shift the conversation to how you can bring in light and divert attention away from the shadow side of the story. Ask your Higher Self to communicate with the Higher Self of the person involved, giving them inner peace, light and love to whatever is not in alignment with their truth.

5. When you find yourself trapped in a toxic environment, see others beyond their fears or shadows. Their victim consciousness is what keeps them in a low field of vibration. Listen, be an observer, detach from their stories and bring light and love. Ask the Ascended Masters to step in and do the healing and create a safe and sacred space between you and others.

6. Don't take other's stories personally. This is Toltec wisdom. When you find yourself in a confrontational situation, remember that the other person has his/her own dream, story or illusion. It is not about yours. Stop, reflect, listen and don't take anything personally. They are expressing what they have inside their own story.

7. Always check in with yourself, what is it within you that attracted this situation? Recognize that the energy that you are feeling is not even your own. Ask, "Where is this energy coming from?"

8. Limit your exposure to your "hot zone" things that trigger and drain your energy. Stay away from large crowds of people who are not peaceful.

9. Be surrounded by likeminded people. Seek mentors and teachers who can give you support in what you are going through. Heal yourself and be empowered. Being an Empath is a gift to help others in what they are going through. Your experiences are to be shared in order to transcend negative and lower vibrations. You are a messenger of love and light for others.

10. Use and focus on a "neutral symbol" that gives you peace when you find that you are with someone that has vampire energy. Perhaps a butterfly, a dove,

moonlight, the ocean. Be in nature, walk and breathe, ground and recharge your energy.

Chakras, Vibrations and Healing

Everything is energy and we are all vibrating in different frequencies. To simplify the mathematical patterns of existence, we need to understand how these principles affect us in our daily lives. The vibrations we hold reflect what we create in our realities. The Third dimension is the dense or physical dimension of this material world, but creation starts from the energetic field of vibrations. We are masters of this creation, co-creating everything that is in our experiences. In order to be a master of our creations for our highest good, we need to understand how the universal laws affect us.

Imagine yourself as a conduit of this universal energy receiving amazing vibrations from this field of light.

In our seven major Chakras system, we have the tools to gauge how we are vibrating in our own system. These vortices of energy vibrate and need to be balanced for the energy and light to flow in a harmonious way. Balanced and harmonious, the chakras unite in a synchronized fashion to integrate the universal energy and light that flows within our subtle energy systems. We will know when something is off, when some aspect of our lives is blocked or stagnant.

There are different aspects of our necessities designed in our Chakras that point us to what we need to shift and release, and the blockages from any Chakra center that is calling us for attention. The Chakras holds the blueprint of our karma and reincarnation. As you evolve, your soul holds the energetic imprints of all your thoughts, emotions, actions and words that you have acquired and done in all timelines, dimensions, space and reality. Can you imagine how vast the information that our Chakras hold is? It sounds like the Akashic Records, the only difference is that Chakras are templates or vortices of energy that govern our system. Akashic Records are in the Akashic field and can be accessible when you desire. The Chakras run the whole system day in and day out. It is the mechanism that keeps the fire burning.

The Akashic Records are the records or map of where your soul has been, present and potential probabilities for your future self. As we face our daily lives, we are triggered by situations that will be in our conscious fields of realities. We have the power to choose. Free will allows us to contract or expand this experience towards our subconscious mind or to gear towards our super conscious mind, a space where we are connected to our infinite True Self. Our conscious mind is the space where we have the choices to make. There is no right or wrong in this process but a continuum of progress of our soul's evolution. As we choose the path of least resistance, we learn that we can evolve in our soul's growth by understanding how our chakras work.

What are the steps for healing our karma in the Akashic Records by using the tools of the Chakras?

1. Observe which Chakra in your system is blocked or stuck. Once identified, know the lessons and Corresponding issues that govern this particular Chakra.

2. Check back on your life story and family history, what kind of patterns and cycles are you experiencing? What kind of emotional signatures you are currently experiencing?

3. This will lead you to the antidote of what your karma is teaching you. The triggers in your life are the teachers that allow you to increase your frequency of light or elevate your life.

4. Look at the bigger picture and how your soul's perspective can shift you into accepting circumstances in your life. How you can love yourself unconditionally and be an evolved sentient being.

5. Balance, clear and release these patterns, the conditioning and energies in your Akashic Records. Ask the Lords of the Akashic Records to assist you in your ascension process. Surround yourself with the Ascended

Masters, Archangels and angels, your spiritual teams and guides, Higher Self and body Deva spirit to help you transcend this incarnation into your highest good and potential. Be free of your karma.

Letting Go of Responsibilities that are not ours

As we become more mature in our healing journeys, we recognize patterns that are not healthy for us. One of them is being attached to others in co-dependent ways. They can be members of our family, friends, co-workers, strangers or clients that are in our energy fields. The Archetypal energies such as the **Healer, Rescuer and Angel** are mostly affected by these patterns.

As passionate as we can be to serve, rescue and help others to heal and bring them light, we can find ourselves trapped in the illusion of being responsible for others happiness and inner peace. We may be feeling burdened and drained with their predicament and dispositions in life. This is a sign of attachment to the outcome of their soul's path.

These are some questions that will help you in balancing your energies to be a wholesome healer:

1. Am I taking responsibility for someone else's happiness and inner peace?

2. Am I drained and burdened after my session or meeting with this person?

3. What is the root of this? Is this from my childhood?

4. Who represents these people's energy in my family?

5. Do I have unresolved issues with my family members?

6. How do I feel about these emotions?

7. What am I getting from this behavior pattern?

8. What are my lessons from these situations?

9. How can I clear these patterns/behavior?

10. What are the new patterns of behavior that I want to create and embody?

After answering these deep introspective questions from your Akashic Records, you will find some clarity and light in your field. What I discovered is that we all want to be loved. This need, if not received as a child, will manifest as co-dependency when we become adults. What can we do to transform these entanglements? We have to be aware of the vibrations of others who we are relating to. What are their energy signatures? Is it positive or negative? Are they talking about others in a negative way or uplifting others? Do they carry vampire energies? These are signs that you have to be aware of, you will need to protect yourself from being affected and letting them affect you. Because everything is a projection of yourself, until you get the lesson, you will be surrounded by these energies. So learn the lesson and create a new life.

The lessons needed to be learned most are about boundaries, acknowledgment that you wanted to be loved, to get attention and that you felt insecure about yourself. Boundaries are healthy for us to be centered in our energy fields. This makes us feel wholesome because we are not leaking or draining our energies when we have these filters around us. The best way of protection is to surround yourself with a Light that resonates with your frequency. It can be a Blue Ray with **Archangel Michael** or a Violet Flame with **Ascended Master St. Germain and the Violet Flame.** I use this Light to protect myself from any harm before I enter a room, to meet with someone, do a healing session or travel. Any time I feel low or not my highest self, I call these Masters of Light right away in my energy fields. They have the power to give you a strong force field of Light.

When you feel whole, you know that whatever the other person is going through just is. It is their soul's journey and their own process. You are never responsible for their path. You are there to be the observer and to bring Light back to their focus which they have forgotten. We are the showers and bringers of Light. Mastery of ourselves is needed to be a powerful and strong force in this paradoxical world of illusions. When you give your Light, it is important to know that you are also receiving blessings from the Source because you are fulfilling your Higher Self's purpose. The more you give Light to others the more you receive gifts in this lifetime.

Being an observer helps you to be detached from the outcome of your service to others. Help those in need with no expectation of return. Act out of love with no reward. These are the light attributes of having these Archetypal energies. Keep yourself light hearted and when you feel drained make sure to ground yourself in nature. The spiritual and healing energies from nature and Mother Earth are important for the manifestation of our Higher Selves. Because we are receivers or conduits of these Light frequencies, we need to understand that grounding these high frequency energies is a must, in order to be balanced and grounded in our healing.

Be focused and clear on your heart's desires and soul's purpose. Know that whatever is in your field can be transformed and healed. When someone is in your field, it is a gift for you to receive. Receive with an open heart, listening to the messages of your spiritual guides and teams. Let go of things that do not work for you. Know that everything passes away. Be gentle with yourself. Let go of the burdens that you have put on yourself. Create a new pattern of self-love and empowerment. Know that you are always loved, supported by the Universe and the Source of all that is.

Opening and healing our heart requires a deep look into our soul's perspective on what is going on with our current situation. It is taking inventory of our life story. Where we are right now and what do we think we should be? This is about being true and authentic to our own selves, feeling our emotions in our deepest core being. No denial, no doubt and no fear, but purely taking that big leap of faith in awakening our hearts and allowing this space of beckoning our soul's calling.

There are significant blockages or patterns that we are creating when we experience brokenness. What really are the deeper roots underlying the walls around our heart? It is not easy to pinpoint, especially if we have the tendency to blame others for the failure of our relationships. Take a moment to be detached from the other party and pay attention to yourself, ask these questions in your Akashic Records and they will help you open your heart's wisdom.

Murder or suicide in the family can intensify suffering from pain, anger, revenge, resentment, rejection, abandonment, betrayal and many other emotions that are not healthy for us. We are here to transcend this experience. We are the karma healers. We are the light bearers of our lineage. We clear the path for our generations to come with love and light. This is an important process of clearing the karma of our ancestors.

The Masters of Light will help us attain our soul healing when we open our Akashic Records to review, see, and know what patterns are kept within our heritage. The gatekeepers guide us in our ascension process to help us accelerate our growth towards wholeness. We then see the bigger picture of our lives. Free will is always ours. We now choose and learn from our lessons. When we understand, we become more aware, awake and enlightened about the effects of our thoughts, words, emotions, intentions and actions. We realize that all of these have bearing on our written Records. We become responsible for all of our conscious choices. Destiny is in our hands and we are governed by universal laws.

Steps to heal the karma bondage in our family:

1. Open your Akashic Records. You can do this by yourself or by going for a consultation.

2. When you open your book of life. Go into your heart space and forgive yourself and others who have hurt you in this lifetime. State this: "I forgive myself for hurting others and I forgive others for hurting me consciously or unconsciously in all timelines, dimensions, space and reality. And so it is." Envision these people and feel the patterns that are being revealed to you. Heavy emotions vibrate in lower frequencies like resentment, judgment, anger, abandonment, rejection, and many others. These are the patterns of your karma, toxic to your life. As you probe further, you can also have visions of other past lives you have lived. Remember the feelings

that were triggered. They are the messages that are being revealed to you by the gate keepers.

3. Now it is time to release. Ask St. Germain and the Violet Flame to assist you. "St. Germain and the Violet Flame, please transmute all these energies that are not of light, name them: _____. I ask that these energies go back to the Source of love and light. Please infuse the void with unconditional love, forgiveness, compassion, kindness, abundance, inner peace, joy and bliss. (Add anything that you would love to bring into your life) Thank you, thank you, and thank you. And so it is."

4. Close the Akashic Records. Thank the Lords of the Akashic Records for allowing you to have a glimpse of your Records. Now, close your book of life. It is very important to close your Records. "The Records are now closed, the Records are now closed and the Records are now closed."

As you learn and acknowledge the karmic bonds that you inherited from your family, it is time to heal them in your Akashic Records. This is a multi-dimensional healing tool. All layers of your mental, emotional, etheric and astral bodies become clear in your book of life. We are releasing these patterns in all timeline, dimensions, space and reality. Ask the Ascended Masters to clear these and heal. Ask these energies to go back to the Source of love and light. When we clear these energies, we need to ask the Masters of Light to infuse love, peace, grace or any blessings that you would love to have.

Prayer:

"I ask the Lords of the Akashic Records to open my book of life and allow access to my own Records. My name is _____(state your legal name) The Records are now open.

(Repeat three times) I ask that my family's karmic bondage and energetic imprints in my book of life be cleared, released and healed. I ask these energies to go back to the Source of love and light. I ask the Archangels and angels to infuse the healing light and essence within my cellular level of memories, consciousness and existence. Thank you, thank you and thank you for this healing. My Akashic Records are now closed, they are now closed, they are now closed. And so it is. "

We are living in challenging times. Tremendous chaos surrounds us. What do we do to assist in alleviating the pain of our human consciousness? We have to be conscious of our own weaknesses, karma, bondages, blockages, hooks, cords, and temptations. Without knowing our own shadows, we are unable to pinpoint what areas need light.

We have freewill. Through our choices, we veer towards light or darkness. If we do not wake up in this incarnation, we are going to continue living on the wheel of karma. Our patterns are not going to shift. We are perpetuating the same suffering in our collective unconscious. It is time to rise up, to take the lead, to have courage to move forward. Have faith and totally surrender to your calling. Heed the call and see the signs evident around us. The doors open, the veil is lifted for those who seek.

Inner Mastery of Our Soul

Inner Mastery of Our Soul

What is inner mastery? It is connecting and listening within yourself and your soul. In this space, there is no separation between your ego and soul. In this space, we are one with the spirit that resides within this physical body of ours. We are bigger than this body, we are multi-dimensional beings of light and love. When we are attune to these high frequencies of love and light, we become aligned to our blueprints, we master our soul's path. We do not waste our time and energy. We only allow things that will serve our highest selves. We are sensitive and vulnerable to the energy fields. It is however imperative that we make sure that we are centered, balanced and focused on what we want to create in our universe. We are the vibrations and energy that people long to be with full of light and love.

Living in this paradoxical world can make you confused with your directions. Be in your heart space. Be still and meditate. Listening to your inner guidance, you become aligned with who you truly are, the authentic self that you are being called to be. You are given this one lifetime right here right now. Create the most beautiful expression of yourself in this world.

Ask questions that will open your mind to the vast expansive universe that we live in. By asking we receive answers from the creative force of our Source of all that is. Pay respect to everything living and non-living that assist you on your path to freedom. Free yourself of attachments from people, things and places that you inhabit. They are impermanent and uncertain of results. Release any expectations that will breed resentment. Free and be. You are an observer of your creations. See what kind of vibrations you are bringing into yourself and others. This will calibrate you into your true happiness and inner peace.

Being a master of your inner self brings you into oneness. This is the unified consciousness when one is allowing the space of be. We are here to witness the grandeur creation of the universe. Be that light that penetrates the veil within and attune to your intuition. Be the conduit of this creative force to flow this expression of your Self into the universe. You are one with the divine creation, you are the co-creator of this energy fields. Manifest your mastery, humbly surrendering to this force of life the gifts that we inherit from our ancestors. We become the hands of God, the one that reaches out to those who need to see their magnificence and shine. Light up this world with so much love, hope and faith that we will all find fulfillment of our existence with deep reverence to life and be unified with all sentient beings of light. We are the masters of all creation, be one with all that is.

33 Blockages of Manifesting Abundance

Our collective consciousness is unconsciously encoded with fear templates and these templates have been running within our psyche, energy fields and souls forever as we live in this third dimension. The power, manipulations and control that run our government, school systems, banking systems, churches and other social structural institutions are based on this fear agenda for gain and to manipulate the way we think and respond to crises. We are blinded by this conspiracy and we are now awakening from our long sleep. Healing scarcity is a huge part of our clearing and healing these unconscious negative belief systems, patterns and conditioning that we inherited right from the get-go. We are also looking at our multi-dimensional energy fields when we are healing this blockage of lack.

As I become an evolved Akashic Records healer, I've tapped into these blockages and found ways to open the gates of abundance in my own life and others. I'm on fire to share these codes with others to help our humanity evolve as sentient beings of love and light. When we want to create, we first have to know and acknowledge what the blockages are in our creation. We then recognize these and clear them from our energy fields. Our energy field is comprised of layers namely: physical, mental, emotional, etheric and astral fields. We are looking at all the disturbances that were created from these planes.

What are these blockages?

1. Ancient lineage, bloodline and DNA, that is inherited from our lineage. We have to realize that the beliefs, conditioning and patterns that we have carried from all of these dimensions are unconscious negative beliefs that we have imprinted in our mental, emotional, physical and spiritual fields.

2. Past life karmas and bondages.

3. Vows, contracts and agreements of poverty from past lives.

4. Archetypes of the beggar, monk, priest and nun.

5. Insecurity related to low self-esteem.

6. Non-forgiveness towards parents or others.

7. Unconscious negative beliefs about money.

8. Fear of success or failure.

9. False beliefs of not deserving.

10. If you are spiritual you are not supposed to have money.

11. Money is the root of evil.

12. You have been traumatized regarding the issue of money.

13. Sacral chakra is closed, sexual abuse experience.

14. Root chakra is not grounded, and feelings of not belonging here on mother earth.

15. Physical clutter around the house.

16. Procrastination.

17. Inconsistency with words and actions.

18. Broken promises, no integrity.

19. Takers not givers, greed.

20. Taking things that are not yours.

21. Rich people are evil.

22. Heart chakra blocked, broken hearted.

23. I'm all alone.

24. Money is punishment.

25. Money is taken away from me when I have it.

26. Thinking small about ourselves.

27. Body is heavy and dense.

28. Mind is scattered, no focus.

29. Intentions to harm others.

30. Attachment to lack.

31. Consumed with worries and fear.

32. Stubbornness.

33. Not open to possibilities, thinking inside the box.

How can we clear these blockages?

All the blockages that are mentioned here can be cleared with a multi-dimensional healer. We are healing beyond this physical dimension, energies, timelines and realities. Our Akashic Records hold the blueprints of our souls, here in the hologram of our soul's matrix we can intervene and be guided with the assistance of our Ascended Masters, Archangels and angels, our spiritual teams and guides, loved ones and ancestors from other dimensions and benevolent beings of love and light. To create is to manifest our Higher Self in this incarnation, tapping into the universal energy.

By clearing our energy fields, we are re-calibrating our existence into our multi-dimensional self. In creation, we are tapping into the universal energy. To expand our mind and heart, we have to align all our chakra energy centers. Creation comes from co-creating with the divine Source or God. In this expansive motion, creation is in the universal fields. It has to start from that space of intention. As we forecast our intention to the universe, it creates the Law of Attraction. Attracting things, people and places to us to fulfill our dreams and projects.

Visualize your dreams. They are already here within your reach and within you. Then, put your attention to your dreams, and focus on your creative expression. With action, create steps towards your project; collaborate with likeminded people who vibrate in love and light. Surrender totally to the divine source with trust and faith, knowing that it is already given. You are the receiver of these blessings.

Be grateful for what you have, that is the key to abundance. Open your heart and mind to receiving gifts from the universe. This is your birthright, share your gifts and service to others and you will receive abundance. Receiving and giving is one unified and strong force field in creation.

Sacred prayer:

"I totally surrender to the Source or God, all my attachments to things, people and places that are not serving my highest good. I now release, clear and heal all blockages from my being, from my physical, mental, emotional, etheric and astral bodies. I ask for forgiveness for having hurt my Self and others. I forgive those who have harmed me consciously and unconsciously in all timelines, dimensions, space and realities. I have faith and trust that it is my divine birthright to live an abundant, healthy and successful life. And so it is."

The Integration of our Shadows and Light

We live in a paradoxical world, we have shadows and we are light. They are the opposites of each other but they are our guideposts to our wholeness when we learn the secrets of being an alchemist. We are given this wisdom to turn lead into gold. Our seeming problems are actually our leads to our highest potential. We will find empowerment, inner peace, fulfillment and happiness when we are in the space of this quantum leap; taking any shadows or darkest nights of our souls as portals ready to illuminate our consciousness. Our harmonious space will come from integrating these different aspects of our spectrum. We are light, we have different shades of color, and we are like these colors living in all different hues and waves of particles. We can only see what is refracted in our light benders but the universal energy fields are multi-dimensional and there is more than our physical eyes can see. Our shadows are lower vibrations that are coming from fear. We need to see ourselves beyond this physical dimension; we have to shift our perception on how we can see beyond the shadows of our experiences.

When we are in the dark, we are in the lower vibrations of our emotional body. We are energetically imprinted within our DNA by our ancient lineage, bloodline and family's negative unconscious beliefs, patterns and conditioning. We get attached to the negative aspect of our situations. We cannot see beyond the shadows of our challenges. The challenge is to see beyond the problems and commit to the integrity of our soul, the light aspect of our being. We are put into challenges to rise up beyond our human capabilities. We are the alchemists of our own destiny. We can co-create with the universal energy. We are just too stubborn to bend our own ways of thinking. It is high time to unlearn all our beliefs, patterns and conditioning of how small we think we are.

We are in the collective consciousness of humanity. The quantum shift is here. However, we first have to acknowledge that we are a part of all that is. The shadows are energetic imprints from our unconscious mind. The Light is the true essence of our soul's dimension. When we know that we are bigger than this physical incarnation, we can establish a new template that our challenges are disguises, here to fully open our mind and hearts to see beyond the form. Problems are illusions of our unconscious mind. As we unfold the trappings of these challenges, we become the observer of our new realities. We witness our shifts and changes that are occurring in our parallel universe. As we shift, the wave particles in our brain cells create new neurological pathways that produce our new realities.

These pathways are our guides towards our new self and to new ascension patterns for our emotions and mental thoughts. We are creating new paradigms in the way we think and act. Our emotions are guided with a new vibrational frequency of sound and light.

We become lighter in our thinking, aligned to our multi-dimensional state of existence. We become the alchemist of our soul's mastery. We come here to experience being human and then transcend our victim consciousness into empowerment. We are here to share this new foundation to our collective consciousness, in order to assist the ascension of our humanity's evolution of consciousness. We are responsible for all our thoughts, words, emotions and actions that are duly recorded in our Akashic Records. We are accountable for the vibrations that we hold energetically.

Our souls have mental, physical, emotional, etheric and astral bodies. We have to clear the debris and toxins that we accumulate in our energetic body to function at our highest. We can clear, release and heal all those vibrations that are not serving our highest potential. They are judgments that we put into our own selves out of our own insecurity. We have to be in the purest Light of vibrations. Our goal is to become a clear conduit for the Masters of Light to attune us with our highest good. Whatever you are carrying will unfold the Light aspects of your shadows. There is only fear and Love. Light is the answer to the shadows. When we become honest and face our fears then we shine this pure Light within us. The shadows dissipate and we step out of the darkness. We release these densities, attached shadows, thus fear can no longer take place because Light is upon us. We connect with the Ascended Masters that guide us. The angelic messages or whispers are now pronounced and all we have to do is listen. Be still and know that you are loved.

The **High Councils of Light** are here to remind us of our pure Light, our Soul's dimension. We connect to our Higher Self, aligned with the ancient wisdom of our land, standing to honor existence, to make a difference in our relationships and to be a Light in our universe. We are being called to radiate this Light into the darkness, in order to uphold truth. We must be true to ourselves. We can only shine when the shadows dissipate. Are you ready to take these challenges into victory? We are the alchemists, victors of this world of darkness. Take courage. Bring in your armor of Light. Be the warrior of Light, there is no more fear but Light that surpasses all understanding. This is the true armor. We are protected and guided in this field of darkness and light. These are the tools of spirituality. Do good things and let that shining light be your guide in all aspects of relationship. Let there be Light. Know you are the Light of this universe.

Our Heart's Essence

In this time of awakening, we open our heart's portals and receive healing light from our higher consciousness and Masters of Light. We become aware of our expansive selves beyond this physical dimension. Our senses are heightened with limitless energy, vibrations and different bands and waves of frequencies that abound to our universal energy. We become conduits of light, energy and love. We can transform any shadow, negative energy and blockages instantaneously with no boundaries and confinements of time and space. This universal energy is boundless and abundant. Our hearts are the portals to receive this in our existence and can store these electro-magnetically amplified vibrations. When someone is aware of the living entity that is your awareness, you attract situations and people that resonate with your vibration. Like attracts like. We are living in paradox; the shadows are here to shift our consciousness into light.

Finding the key to this treasure is the secret to happiness. When we are going through difficulties and conflicts, find the pattern, name the shadow or conflict, look within and realize that this shadow is a part of you. Ask this egoic shadow, "What are you here to teach me?" Embrace and bring in the positive aspect of light nature to the darkness. You will shift the situation into the light perspective of your Soul. Our hearts hold the vibration of truth. Truth is relative to the experience of the observer. When you feel the truth, your whole sense of being vibrates light. There is a resonance to your Higher Self. You feel in alignment with your authentic self. You feel freedom in your expression and liberated from what others think of you. You connect to your deep insights and emotions. It is your authentic self that will lead the way to your own truth. Be yourself and know that it is your soul's journey. Be aware of how you spend your present moment. Become open to the infinite possibilities that are here for you. It is your birth right; you are the spark of the universal energy. When we understand this magnificent aspect of our existence, we become attuned to our gifts and become aware of our creations.

Connect to your heart's essence and ask questions that will lead you to your truth. When you connect to your heart, you become alive and vibrant. You have that force within you that ignites the fire of your spirit. Our hearts are vast and expansive vortices of energy. When it vibrates in truth it can touch infinite amount of souls instantaneously. We are living in matrix fields that have no boundaries to what it can contain. Begin shining your bright light emanating from your heart. Shower your life with love for yourself and others. It is the strongest force in the universe. It binds us with compassion for all sentient beings of light. We are light and a mirror of each other's light when we are open to receiving the gifts of the Universe.

Listening to your heart is an important practice that will align you with your soul's purpose. Ask the Masters of Light to recalibrate and activate your inner ears to be able to listen to the messages of the spirit. They are quite subtle and soft, giving us shivers in our skin and knowing that we are tapping into the deepest truth of our essence. Open your senses to receive these subtle nudges from the spirit of our hearts; they will align you with your highest potential. In our heart's fields there could be energetic walls that separate us from being intimate and open with others. Ask your heart, "Where are these walls coming from? And how can I take them down?" Your heart will show you the answers and ways to slowly release these stuck energies around it. They will reveal the answers within your conscious mind and create an expansion in your heart's space.

What Hurts Will Make Us Whole

Have you thought of those emotions that separate you from another person? Those are the things that hurt us the most. We try to deny them or blame the other person, but truly those things that hurt us are the things that will point us back to becoming whole again. They are the triggers of our fragmented selves. When we got hurt in the past, we buried these feelings deep inside us and became numb. We built walls around our hearts and it is not easy to open these thick walls again. It will take a situation that will trigger us and trigger our emotional body. Our vulnerability will surface and we will be in a fog. Questioning our intimacy and trust, we wonder, is it safe to be here or be with this person? We are so good at running away from our own creations. We run away for fear of being hurt or hurting others. Let us open our hearts and minds to what is being presented to us. This situation is asking us to listen and let go of ego. We are not separated from the other person. We are one.

To enter into this space of oneness one must know this wisdom and believe that we can get this act together to create a world free of the cycle of karma. We are here to experience, to open our hearts and to be at one with the divine creations and receive grace. When we are experiencing challenges, the situations are asking us to humble ourselves. Should we become defensive, we close our hearts to each other, pretending that everything is good. In the midst of this, we create assumptions in our heads and thus bring us more stress and separation.

If we believe everything is energy, then whatever we are hiding is seen and felt by the other person. Let us not be blind to all of our creations. Let us be open, honest and vulnerable. It takes courage to be this new person. We are bombarded by chaos and lies and it takes willpower to choose wisely. Know that whatever is in front of you is your creation. Then, you can come to that place of forgiveness and allow the energy of love and light to take hold in your fields. This will dissipate fear, and will give you the courage to face the truth. There is no separation. There is only oneness. We are one.

The other person's suffering is ours as well. Let us be compassionate and allow the divine grace to fill our hearts, body, mind and soul. Let us humble our Self and be at peace. Together, we can change the way we think, our perceptions will flow in a new direction towards peace and unified consciousness. We can collaborate and create a peaceful world. We are the answer to all our seeming problems. When we see them as opportunities to open our hearts, we become the alchemists of our shadows. We have the power to transmute anything that is not light. We are given this truth to be at peace within and as we practice this new pattern of thought, we will shift our consciousness.

We can only solve our problems by shifting within and knowing that we are given this tool to change the way we see things coming from oneness. Each of us can be an instrument of peace; where there is separation, let us be whole and be free of our own egotistic mind. Let us free ourselves from pointing out to others what we want to see within ourselves. Let us be at peace. We cannot wait for others but it can start now within us.

Create your highest and best version of yourself. Be who you are, authentic in all ways. Remember what hurts you will bring you wholeness. Be open and express yourself to the other person to create peace and love for all. Let go of fear and illusions. Be present and allow the divine grace to channel through you these gifts of healing.

Steps in Releasing Toxic Emotions

We are entangled in chaotic times with the rest of humanity. Our collective unconscious is overwhelmed with fear, anger and despair. Unhealthy emotions lead to stress, illness and death. Our thoughts run from unconscious negative thoughts and beliefs that we have inherited since the beginning. All of these blockages make us stuck in a space where we cannot shine the light that is our true essence. We become attached to our mundane lives without putting an importance on our contribution as a conscious universal being of light and love.

What are the emotions that you are expressing in your own little world?

This will affect the people around you and our whole humanity's collective consciousness. We are universal and expansive yet we forget how powerful we are. We have attachments to the illusions that our material world is what is important. We have to attune to our spirit and be clear about what are we contributing to this world.

Are you creating a beautiful expression of yourself? The beauty and love that we give and receive is an expression of divine light in our awareness. When we vibrate in a lower frequency of our emotional and mental field, we attract conflicts, pain and drama. We are the magnet of our creations.

How can we liberate ourselves from these blockages?

First, we have to acknowledge that we have a problem. When you want to change something, it is crucial that you acknowledge what you want to shift. Shifting your reality starts by realizing that you are responsible for your vibrations. Once realized, you become the observer of your thoughts and emotions. This creates an awareness of your energy fields. We are all energy, one body and one soul. The universal energy is what we are tapping into. Once we become aware of this concept, we know that when we hurt others we hurt our own selves. We are part of the whole.

Every aspect of our being needs to be aligned to our highest good and the highest good of all. What is our highest potential? We all want to live peacefully and be happy. We all want to help raise the vibrations of our collective consciousness.

By going within, we can start to shift our external realities. Everything that we see is a mirror of ourselves. We live in a holographic universe. Open your eyes to the truth of what is presented to you. It is a trigger because it wants to change. Listen to the nudges of your heart. Merge your mind and heart when creating a decision. Tap into your awareness and be expansive. Do not judge others as it hurts your core being. We are one.

Why Do We Attract Our Opposites

Do you ask why we attract people that are totally opposite of who we are? We magnetize these in our fields because deep within ourselves there is something that we need to integrate. Like the Yin and Yang of life, we are here to experience light and shadow. When we are able to assimilate the lesson, we become one with the other person or ourselves.

How to integrate the lessons in life

1. Observe what the contrasts are in your life right now. Name them. These are the shadows that are not working for you, or things that the other person brings into the relationship. They may be character or things that agitate you. These are triggers or catalysts that require your attention.

2. Once named, it is time to investigate, ask questions that will connect you to the missing link of the bigger picture. Go back to your childhood. Who does this person remind you of?

3. What kinds of emotions are created from your interactions? Is it coming from fear or love?

4. What separates or divides you from this person? Name the qualities, character and describe in more details.

5. Journal your experiences with the other person. Ask your Akashic Records questions to assists you in your healing.

6. Align yourself; be congruent with your mind and heart. You will find that the other person is here to remind you of the things that you have not accepted about yourself.

7. When we have self-acceptance, we become open and things usually do not trigger us anymore. We react less and know that whatever this person is carrying is about them and not you. You become empowered and wholesome.

8. The opposite of the shadow is light. Turn the contrast into clarity. Put your attention to light and positive energy. Create from this space.

9. In the alchemy of life, see the lead and turn into gold by knowing that you are the alchemist and have the power to do this.

10. Be at peace within and with others. The shadows become a part of you and no longer separate you from who you truly are, a bright light.

What are the steps in releasing toxic emotions?

1. Acknowledge you have a problem. You are the magnet of your reality.

2. Go into your heart space. Breathe. Remove yourself from situations that trigger you. Reflect within.

3. Listen to your mind or ego, what is it saying to you? Now listen to your heart, what is it telling you?

4. When you become aware of their dialogue, you can start to differentiate what makes sense and what touches your heart.

5. Remember that the other person is in his/her own world. You have your own illusions as well. The time has come to collide when there is a trigger. This is also a time to have space and recollect your mental thoughts and emotions.

6. Your body will talk to you. Tears will appear and it is a sign that you are releasing old paradigms or old wounds of the soul. Listen and stay still.

7. When your thoughts and emotions are integrated, forgive the other person and reconcile.

8. Create a beautiful and loving space for you and the other person to bond.

9. Light a candle. Thank God or Source for giving this harmony and love between you and the other person.

10. Remember this time to commemorate your rebirth and how you had surrendered to the merging of your ego and soul.

What do you do when you feel powerless?

Life can present us with challenges. Whatever we are being called to face with fearlessness, with courage we have the intention to create peace, light, and love. But how can we see this path when we are in the middle of it? This is the work of seeing clearly that this seeming problem is actually a door of opportunity to expand our perceptions on what really is here and how can we shift this into becoming a positive situation.

First, we have to come from the perspective that we are powerful over all challenges. We are given the spiritual tools to give light to any darkness. We are light workers. This shadow is a cry for help. Coming from this perspective, we become a spiritual warrior of the light. We are here to transcend any obstacles that come our way. We are powerful beyond our imagination. We simply need the right perception on how we can see things that don't seem light.

Steps in being powerful:

1. Acknowledge the problem. Be clear on what is being presented.

2. Check in with yourself. Questions to ask:

-Is there anything that I contributed to this conflict? Where am I draining my power? Was my boundary crossed?

-Am I projecting? Am I blaming? Am I in control? These questions can help in your inquiry.

3. You are the magnet to every situation, face the situation with an open mind and open heart.

4. Check which "Archetypes" are being animated? This will help you not take the situation personally. Thus, you will not react to the person's behavior knowing that these are Sacred Contracts.

5. After naming the Archetypes, ask for the lesson or roles that need to be integrated for your highest good and others.

6. Take the other person's reactions as her/his own Archetype in action not yours.

7. You can't fix or change the other person, however, take responsibility of your contribution.

8. Be in your sacred space, reflect and send light and love to the other party.

9. Know that there is a Higher Power; surrender the things that you cannot change.

10. Allow things to unfold with divine timing. Everything passes away. Have faith, forgive and empower yourself knowing that challenges are here to open you up, expand and see things in a different light.

Prayer:

"Divine guidance leads me towards peace, light, and love. May I see what is presented to me as my own shadows reflected back to me. Give me the humility to forgive my Self and others. Let me be an instrument to channel grace to others who are lost. It is your guiding voice that I will hear within my heart to create a space that will give us harmony and power to bring in the true light of freedom. Let us free ourselves from the shackles of darkness and confusion. Let there be light and love in our midst. We surrender to you our challenges and that we may find peace with all our emotions and mental thoughts. We are powerful light beings and we thank you for this grace. Thank you, thank you and thank you. Let it be done with effortless, ease, love and grace. And so it is. "

Embracing Our Shadows

We have shadows in our lifetime because we are not fully in our spirit body. We are multi-dimensional. We have our physical, emotional, mental, etheric, and astral bodies. Shadows are part of our light, we are here to discover these shadows and reverse them so to speak. When we see the opposite of our shadows, then we can integrate our light within. It is an alchemical process. We can integrate our shadows and light together to attune with the best version of ourselves.

It is a challenge to see beyond the shadow because it has a life of its own. When we are in the dark, it consumes us, we get stuck and it feels like we are trapped inside the box. The way to uplift ourselves is to turn this situation around and see the positive aspects of the trigger. For example, you may feel like you are rejected by others, so you know that rejection is the trigger. Look beyond the situation and see where the patterns of rejection started in this lifetime.

We form our foundational beliefs between the ages of infancy and 7, so it is important to reflect and really do your archetypal inner child healing. When you find the pattern, usually the person reminds you of the character who rejected you in the past. Now, if you have not done the process of forgiveness, this is the time to let go. Go into your heart space and forgive yourself and others. This is a beautiful prayer of forgiveness that we do when we open our Akashic Records.

"I forgive myself for hurting others consciously and unconsciously in this lifetime, all timelines, dimensions, space, and reality. I forgive others for hurting me consciously and unconsciously in this lifetime, all timelines, dimensions, space, and reality. And so it is."

This prayer helps us to clear our energy systems and be light on our path. Non-forgiveness issues are unhealthy; they are toxins in our system. We cannot move forward with unresolved issues, we feel burdened and our energy is attached to lower emotions such as resentment, anger, and judgment.

We have to know our shadows, check where they came from and embrace these shadows by being light on our Self and others. Have compassion and kindness; know that we are here with our shadows and that we have the power to transcend anything. Be an alchemist, turn lead into gold. Your life is mysterious. Live by being aware of your own shadows, reflect, forgive and let go. Move forward to your new patterns, thinking, conditions and live free of your shadows. Know that they are a part of our humanness but each one of us holds the key to the doors of liberation. You know that you have this within and nothing can disturb you because you are the magician. Live in your magic full of wisdom and joy.

Transmuting the Vibrations of Shame and Guilt

Our collective unconscious has emotional imprints of shame and guilt which vibrate at a low frequency. When we are unaware of these Records in our book of life, we repeat the same cycle of our karmic bondage. This lies deeply within our Soul and in order for us to transcend these low vibrations, we have to clear them in our Akashic Records.

These energetic imprints can come from other timelines and past lives. It can also come from this lifetime when you were abused as a child or adult. Any history of abuse can create these energetic imprints in our soul's vibrations. As a part of the collective unconscious, we have inherited these vibrations right at the beginning of our evolution.

How do we know we are affected by the vibrations of shame and guilt?

We can detect this if we are experiencing fear, addiction, attachments, doubts, negative thoughts about ourselves, darkness, depression, insecurity, conflicts, confusion, jealousy, separation, and many other lower vibrations of our emotions. By becoming aware of our feelings, thoughts, and our spirit, we are able to know that we need some assistance from our Masters of Light through the Soul healers.

What are the steps to clearing these vibrations of shame and guilt in our Akashic Records?

1. Recognize that you have a problem. Without acknowledging this shadow, you are unable to shed a light on the darkness.

2. If you know someone who is a Soul healer, seek help as this is a sacred act.

3. If you are familiar with opening your Akashic Records, you can do this for yourself.

4. Open your Akashic Records. Create a safe and sacred space with your spiritual guides, gatekeeper, Ascended Masters, Archangels and angels, your Higher Self and body deva spirit, and the Lords of the Akashic Records.

5. Consult your guides about past lives that contributed to these emotions of shame and guilt.

6. If you have any visions of your past life, write this down and ask your guides to show or reveal to you information that will help you understand how this past life is relevant to your current situation.

7. Go into your heart space, breathe and ask for forgiveness consciously and unconsciously for hurting others. Forgive those who have hurt you in this lifetime and other timelines. You are clearing your heart chakra from all unconscious and conscious energetic imprints from all timelines.

8. Call Archangel Michael and the Blue Ray to protect you and to cut any cords of attachments to people, places, and things that are not serving your highest good. Ask that these energies go back to the Source of love and light.

9. Call St. Germaine and the Violet Flame to transmute all energies that are not of light. Ask that any energetic imprints of shame and guilt be cleared, released, and healed from your Akashic Records.

10. Thank all the guides that have helped you clear these cords; thank the Lords of the Akashic Records for revealing to you what is needed to be cleared. Now close your Akashic Records, the Records are now closed, the Records are now closed, the Records are now closed, and so it is.

*Always remember to thank and close the Records every time you open them.

Inner Strength Comes From Perseverance

We have big visions for our lifetime. When we dream big, we are given universal challenges to test if we are truly ready to receive these visions. When we receive challenges in our soul's journey, these are the times we are being called to persevere. Not too many of us like this space because we want instant gratification. In our digital revolution, everything is instant. You ask a question, google it. This is how our egoic minds work; we think we can get everything we want in a split second.

Our visions are interlinked with our soul's purpose. This is achieved through testing the strength of our spirit. Our spirit cannot lie. Deep within us there is a space of knowing when we are not congruent with our truth. This is the voice of the spirit that whispers in our ears "you cannot hide." This is a space of vulnerability that we do not want others to see because we are afraid to be judged. This is at the core of humanity. We are in fear of what others think of us if our lives are not perfect in the eyes of society. Do I have a lot of money in the bank? Do I have a big house? Am I pretty or good enough? We put these insecurities on ourselves because of what our society has labeled as successful. We want to belong to that elite group because our ego wants us to exist, to be known and this is what we call self-pride. We are all one in this universal mind, the way to detect if our ego is way out of hand is to reflect, journal, and meditate.

The mind and heart has to align and be congruent with our spirit. When we are not aligned with our vision, we get lost in mundane things. When things get rough, we need to stay balanced and centered. There are universal challenges that we are going to encounter because we are being tested on how strong we are and if we can handle these things. When we ask, we will receive. However, we need to be ready and know that there will be challenges. We live and are governed by universal laws. Like metal, it has to go through fire to create steel. We are being put to the test to know if we are ready.

Put your focus on your vision and intention. This is your blueprint for your manifestation. The first steps are to know our intentions and our vision for our dreams. In order to have laser focus of our destiny, we have to anchor our vision or we can get lost in the strong stormy weather of our lives. Whatever kind of chaos or disturbances that come, know that these too shall pass. We need to be in silence to listen to our spirit. The spirit's voice does not exist in the noise of our head but deep within our heart and soul. Inner strength comes from the perseverance of our spirit. We are given the fruits of our labor when we are patient and persevere.

Perseverance is an important ingredient of a true spiritual warrior!

Courage to Move Forward

When we are in the middle of chaotic times, it is easy to get distracted and out of focus. We are energetic beings and we feel the tension around us because there are no boundaries in space. The wisdom is in knowing the spiritual tools that we can access to create a safe and sacred space for us. We are not alone but we have our Ascended Masters, angels, and spiritual teams and guides to intervene and support us.

First, we have to acknowledge our power is beyond this form. These Masters of Light are here to give us information for our ascension process. Transcending our victim consciousness and shifting our lives into empowerment are necessary steps in our process.

here is chaos, old patterns are burning. Our perception shifts into a new way
‿, creating new conditions and situations.

In our Solar Plexus, which is located in the navel area, lays the vortex of energy that we need to propel us towards trusting ourselves. This vortex allows us to trust our gut feelings, the seat of our wisdom. It stems from trusting our own Self, the underlying root of courage. This is an innate feeling of inner strength that we can get ourselves, from any situation that is not serving our highest good. The frequency of the crystal Citrine can help us attain a higher vibration of believing in ourselves. The yellow ray of the Central sun nurtures, strengthens, and supports us in our path as a spiritual warrior.

Reversing our shadows, we are able to find light beyond the dark night of our soul. Others play an important role in our shifts. People who trigger us are our teachers. We must take the time to reflect, listen, and understand that the contracts we have in our lives are predestined. These are sacred contracts in our Akashic Records. We come here to learn and experience being humans. The highest virtue of being a human is forgiveness. Through this compassionate act, we are able to let go of any attachments that are not good for us. The energetic cords are cut and we have Archangel Michael and the Blue Ray that can help us do this. Invoke his presence and envision this beautiful Blue light around us.

Sacred prayer:

"Thank you for your presence Archangel Michael, please cut any cords of attachments from people, places and things that are not serving my highest good. I ask that these energies return back to the Source of love and light, and so it is."

Trust Your Heart

Our hearts are the wisdom keepers of our souls. When we are attuned to the universal love and truth of why we are here, we are able to resonate with the heart's high frequency of light. It takes a lot of experience to know what our hearts are telling us to do because we get confused with how our mind works. To align our mind with our heart's wisdom is the secret to being content and happy.

What is the difference between the voice of ego and that of the heart? The ego speaks from pain, separation, and fear. The heart speaks softly, from a place of vulnerability and oneness. We live in a busy world, with a hectic mind and doubting heart. Becoming vulnerable is a sign of weakness instead of openness and trust. When we are in a relationship, we try to hide these hidden parts that we consider our "shadows". We fear being judged, insecure, and unloved. These are energetic imprints from our traumatic experiences from the past.

Healing our Heart Chakra is the most sensitive part of all vortex energy therapies because this is where we try to control, hide and put up our walls against others. These blockages and traumas can come from many places; our relationships from parents, siblings, society, even past life contracts and vows. Healing from the Akashic Records brings us the missing links to our bigger picture and why we do things the way we do. With the help of the Records we are able to let go, forgive, and release these energetic imprints from all timelines, dimensions, space, and realities.

We are given the opportunities to review our patterns, sacred contracts, and situations with our soul's perspective to create new patterns, ways, and conditions in handling challenges. Acknowledging assistance from our Higher power, Spiritual teams and guides, Ascended Masters, angels and benevolent beings of Light, we are being supported, guided and loved. Totally surrender your life, mind and heart to this path. Trust your heart and listen to your messengers.

In the heart Chakra, call the Ascended Master Paul the Venetian, Archangel Raphael and Archangel Chamuel to help heal our hearts. Envision the color pink or green. Ask for openness, trust, surrender and faith that you will be able to heal your heart and love.

Sacred Prayer:

"I call upon the Masters of Light to assist me in opening and healing my heart. May I be able to let go of things that do not serve my higher purpose, things that deplete my energy, time, and existence, I ask to gain direction, clear guidance, and understanding of my soul's purpose. I now align myself to the highest version of my life and to serving others. Please fill my heart space with compassion, love, kindness and gentleness towards myself and others. Thank you, and so it is."

What do you really want?

What do you truly want? It is a simple question but difficult to answer if we do not know ourselves. We get influenced by others opinions of ourselves. We forget who we truly are. We get stuck in what we have or what we do not have. These are some distractions that keep us away from what we truly want.

Ask this question, "What do I truly want?" and be in complete silence. Listen to your heart. Write down the things that make you happy. Put them all together. Brainstorm and align these answers to your heart's desires. For example, I liked writing as a child. I loved to journal and play at the beach. I wrote all the things that I am passionate about and the things that made me happy.

Things that make me happy:

Nature, communicating with animals and plants, beach, crystals, candle lights, flowers, healing music, writing and reading, listening to mentors, inspiring and helping others, giving and sharing gifts with others, elders, children, empowerment and supporting others, dancing and singing, creating, painting and travelling.

Find the feelings that are strong, these are my core values:

Creative expression, love, authenticity, integrity, freedom, inspiration, empowerment, belonging, trust

What can I do to put these all together and inspire others?

By putting all the things together that make me happy, I was able to incorporate what I really want in my life. This way, I focus on these things and I do not get distracted by other stuff. I realized my love for writing is number one on my list. So I put my attention to writing, then surrounding myself with the things that I love like crystals, plants and healing music. I am attuned to healing energies and I was able to put this into my consultations with others. Inspiring others to be healers, focusing on what they want to create and be happy, makes me happy.

This is a step towards getting closer to manifesting what you truly want in life. You can create a vision board, visualize that all these things are already here, create and be surrounded with positive energies that will uplift your spirit. Know what you truly want.

Grounding Our Thoughts

Many of us are busy in our heads, thinking and allowing thoughts that are endless. We become scattered and find ourselves without direction. Our thoughts stem from a lot of dynamics. They can be coming from old patterns of being a victim, conditioning from when we were children, old beliefs and unconscious negative thoughts about ourselves. Being clouded with these foggy thoughts can be detrimental to creating the best version of ourselves. How can we still these mindless thoughts?

Steps in grounding our thoughts:

1. Find stillness, meditate daily.

2. Allow these thoughts to pass, observe them as they pass through our mind. Be the observer.

3. Do not judge or resist, just be. Every thought passes away. Do not identify them as your own, they are just thoughts.

4. Attachments to these thoughts are the pitfalls of humankind. We think we are these thoughts. We identify and believe them, as we think, we give them power. Be free.

5. As we practice daily meditation, we become more aware of this freedom from our thoughts. It is important to consistently practice stillness.

6. Journaling our thoughts is a powerful tool for transformation. We can see our progress as we write our thoughts daily.

7. Know that our thoughts have vibrations. When we think negative thoughts and thus become negative, we vibrate in lower frequencies that attract conflicts and chaos.

8. If we want to create amazing experiences, we need to be aware of our thoughts and their vibrations. Calibrate your thoughts.

9. Thoughts that are harmful to ourselves and others are unhealthy for us. Acknowledge their presence and let go of them. The inner critic's voice in our head can be experienced but do not allow or give it power. Know that this is coming from a low point of view. Let go and fill the void with positive thoughts.

10. Open your heart and ground your thoughts. Ask yourself, "Are my thoughts positive? Are they kind and necessary? Are they good for me?" If not, let go and fill the void with beautiful and loving thoughts about yourself and others. Bless instead of curse.

Groundless Mind, Fruitful Soul

When we are in the midst of chaos or conflict, we forget that in order for us to feel safe, we unconsciously grasp at suffering. For some reason of survival, we have unconsciously held on for dear life to our problems. This way of coping is the opposite of what we should be doing. Letting go and surrendering is a challenge for us. Having a groundless mind means, we do not grasp at our illusions or suffering. Whatever is happening just is. It is arising because of so many causes that want our attention. It may be from karma of past lives, wounds that need healing, or our body talking to us.

What is a groundless mind? Like a garden, we need to cultivate the soil of our mind. When the ground is full of weeds, we pull them out to prepare for the seeds to sprout. These seeds are the good thoughts that we instill in our mind. The weeds are the worries, illusions, grasping that we put in our mind when we are experiencing challenges. Because we are only allowing good seeds or thoughts, we become fertile with positive energy.

That allows these seeds to grow effortlessly. Just like our mind, we need to cultivate good thoughts that will produce good emotions and deeds.

When we know and gain the wisdom to practice this consciously, meditating and clearing our mind of illusions, we become a conscious and compassionate sentient being. This is the Buddha nature within us; in a deeper level of understanding, we are now ready to have a groundless mind. This happens when we recognize that this physical dimension is a creation of our mind. We become attuned to the impermanence and uncertainties of this world. We reach a deeper level of understanding that anything that we experience here is an accumulation of our state of being, the past, present or future lives that we are living in. These are the multi-dimensional states of our existence.

Having a groundless mind is like floating in the winds of life. We experience what we are going through but we do not accept this as the only reality. Perhaps we are experiencing an illness, and we accept the fact that our body is telling us that there is misaligned energy in our system. Even though it looks like this challenge will alter our life, there is always a higher perspective of looking at things. Why did this have to happen to us? In this lifetime we are going to experience suffering in many forms. If we have that realization about suffering, we know that anything can happen in this incarnation. It will be a basis or fertile ground to start with in dealing with illness. "This happened because it is calling my attention."

Where we put our attention, energy goes. To be in a state of groundlessness, we have to know that our lives are precious in whatever state or form our body is in. We are sacred sentient beings experiencing humanness. The weaknesses of our physical body can be our soul's inner strength. When we are suffering from illness, we first need to understand that this is a part of being human. We are not exempt from this physical state. When we can accept this, we can move onto where we put our attention: the positive side of life. What can be positive when we are challenged? These challenges are the directions in which our soul longs to go.

The groundless state of mind is the space where we let go and surrender control and manipulation. We can plan our lives but it may not always happen the way we planned it to be. It is by being groundless that we create our soul's stamina. This inner strength transcends physical challenges. This soul becomes the inner compass for our directions. When we fully listen to our soul, we become one integrated being in all aspects of our existence.

The fruitful soul is one that endures the pain of this body and endures its changes to a more meaningful existence. We can turn these challenges into miracles. Perhaps through illness, we can become more compassionate and kind to our Self and others. We gain insight and empathy to the suffering of others. We bond with others through this kindness.

Our lives can look like a kaleidoscope when we take a glimpse of certain formations, turn it around and create a more beautiful form. It is through these soulful eyes that we can see through our suffering. It affords a freedom from being stuck. We are liberated from the suffering of not being able to move forward from the pain.

When we are in this pain body, true kindness can move us beyond our mind to know that there is a reality that we can create, perhaps by donating our time to children or the elderly who are dying in hospice care. Anything can take our ego out of the equation, via being of service. First, relinquish the need to grasp. Open the mind and heart to what is.

"How can I serve others through this pain? How can I benefit others through this?" These are questions to ponder when we are challenged.

Be an observer of the mind. Is it groundless or grasping? Release the need to grasp, allow the energy to move into our chakras or body systems. Notice how the energy flows, meditate daily, and go for a walk in nature to commune with Mother Earth. Find other ways to ground the Self. Eat lightly and play. Allow only good thoughts to come in our spacious and groundless mind. These practices can ease whatever we are going through. They bring fruit to our souls.

We are magnificent beings of Light. Be light to our Self and others. Flow with the river of our consciousness and fly with the wings of love.

How Do We Keep Our Vision Clear?

When we are in the midst of chaos, we forget to stop and go into a gap or space to breathe. Chaos is happening because there is a change that is preparing us to shift. When we see things this way, we are able to release the pressure to be hard on ourselves and others. The key is to keep your cool, breathe and know that everything passes away. There is nothing permanent in this world, but change is a sign for us to move forward or release something that is not working for us anymore.

We are addicted to drama and we create more chaos by resisting shifting our perception towards the change. When we look at other people's mistakes, we get distracted in our own thoughts and perceptions. We get entangled in the drama. We lose our focus on what we truly want to manifest. We get sucked into the other person's journey. It is always their choice to learn the consequences of their actions. It is not our lesson, our participation in this relationship is to bear witness and support them for their highest good. Let go of expectations for their choices. When we totally surrender our control in this power struggle, we let go of the hooks and feel lighter. Our relationship vibrates in a higher level of freedom and forgiveness. We become one in spirit.

What are the signs that you are hooked into other people's problems?

1. You find yourself blaming and judging the other person for their choices.

2. You feel anxious and restless.

3. You feel resentment and rejection from the other person.

4. You are entangled in their actions and you react emotionally.

5. You justify your judgments and you find yourself defending the need to be right.

6. You have no boundaries.

7. You feel disrespected and hurt.

These are some signs that you need to be aware of when you are going through some chaos and know that you can still help yourself out of this situation. First, acknowledge that you are entangled. Create boundaries for yourself and others. Filter your thoughts and calibrate your emotions. Center your Self, focus on your positive visions. Do not let other people's situations affect your inner peace. Let go of expectations, control and surrender to the things that you cannot change. Be at peace.

When Your Attachments Are Shaken

In our journeys, we will experience our own inner earthquakes. All our attachments to our roles, jobs, things, and people that we surround ourselves with suddenly are being taken away. We are shaken to the core and we become scattered. We lose our focus. How can we put our attention on the things that work for us? These are universal challenges, we are being tested on how much we can handle. Things that are given to us are here to teach us lessons.

How do we keep our cool? When things around us are collapsing, it is a sign that we are going through rebirth. We are releasing things that do not work for us anymore. We are creating space for a new pattern to exist. Whatever changes are presented, take it as openings. See beyond the ups and downs, it is a part of the cycle of nature. The more we resist, the more it persists. Let go of resistance. Flow with the knowing that everything passes away, we are impermanent. There is no certainty in this transient world. Be an observer of what is transpiring without attachment to the form. Be fluid like the water in the vast ocean, flow with life.

How to keep your cool:

1. Attachments are hindrances to the freedom of our spirit. We attach ourselves to feel like we belong, to gain attention and to be seen.

2. When these attachments are taken away, we lose our false identity. We are off center and we get lost in our thoughts and emotions.

3. We get scared of our loss and fear sets in. We are afraid that we do not matter anymore to our friends and family. We feel like a failure. We are broken inside. Something was taken away and we are not the same.

4. We need to get grounded in our thoughts. Meditate and journal your way through your loss. Every time you lose something, a part of you is taken away. It is a process, do not hurry your way out of this but take your time and be an observer of your thoughts.

5. These are the challenges of our times. Everything passes away. Let go of judgments of yourself and others.

6. Do not be hard on yourself, take time to relax and walk in nature.

7. We recreate our fears. Take an inventory of your story and see where this is rooted from the beginning.

8. When you find the roots of your story, you are able to release this in your Akashic Records and evolve.

9. As we learn our lessons, we ascend. We needed to let go of the stories of being a victim and ponder how we can empower ourselves through these challenges.

10. Be free and let your spirit soar high. We are here to experience life; with its ups and downs we are able to create something beautiful for ourselves and others. Be grateful for all the blessings that you have and be happy.

Betraying Yourself

You wonder where you went wrong. You think of the past, think of the times that were good, yet they do not sum up to what you are feeling right now. The emotions of sadness and being alone arise during the pinnacle of your success. Why? You asked and no thoughts come up. Your heart is like a deep well, deep but dry. You try hard to reach to the bottom of the well and there is nothing, no water, no answer. You are alone, in the height of your success.

Life is a journey of paradox. I believe we are given the duality of life to keep us grounded here on mother earth. We are asked to be humble, to reflect, and go back to our retreat with God. The universe gives us what we need to see and what we need to be grateful for.

You are never alone. Your guides and loved ones from other dimensions are always around you. My mother is my spiritual guide, she comes in times of challenge, and she fills up my heart when I am broken. She knows me better than anybody else. We are connected in eternal time.

People around me are suffering, loved ones, friends and strangers. How can I feel elated when I am in the midst of chaos and suffering? This gives me a bigger picture of the world we live in right now. We try to find inner peace in our home but other countries around us are suffering. How do you find solace? It is in communing with God that you get back to the core of your being. No one in this world can fill that space. Others find solace in meditation, hiding their chaos in stillness of the mind. But this will not suffice, there is something missing. Our soul longs to communicate with God, to directly say "Why do I feel alone?"

Only then, our hearts will open to listen. It is an opportune time to truly be here in the presence of confusion. To be a voice of your true feelings might hurt others but if you keep this to yourself it is toxic. Be true to yourself. Do not betray your own self. Do not allow distractions to penetrate your stillness. Allowing poison to seep through depletes your spirit. Open your heart and ask, be vulnerable, be open.

I have learned one thing for sure, to not have any expectations. Do not expect that your loved ones will be there for you. Sometimes, your loved ones are the ones that hurt you. Because you are intimate, they break open your heart. This is the beauty of life, when we are raw. There are no hidden feelings, let go and know that like clouds in the clear sky, this too, will pass. God's love is here with you no matter what. You are never alone. Never betrayed.

The sweet lesson of abandonment is about you adopting your self. It's time to let go of things that do not work for you. Feel free. You are here to experience life in its fullest; ups and downs are part of this journey. Please be open to fully love and be hurt. Be true to your feelings that no one is there for you. Within you, feel your heart breaking, with this, you may find opening. Allow this fresh air of love, like a new leaf to turn. You are important in the scheme of things. You are never alone; you are always with God, in God. Beloved, you are loved!

Permission to Shine

Do you ever wonder why you are not doing what you are meant to be doing? What stops you from achieving things that make you happy? In this lifetime, you will come into a space where you are ready to take that leap of faith. You will know that when the universe closes a door, another door opens for you. The things that stop you from moving forward are from your old self. This is coming from fear of survival and attachments to "What if?" We are conditioned in old patterns of control and manipulation. The inner critic speaks: "You are not good enough. Who would believe you and who do you think you are?" These are some of the voices of the inner critic that will challenge you in choosing a new way of thinking and living.

In order for us to move forward, we have to be ready and bold to take a risk. Life is full of risks, we are uncertain of our life and death. We will never know when our time to die is, so why not take a risk? Our experiences are what life is all about. There are no failures but learning curves to know what feels right for us or not. Change the current of your lifetime, if it does not go that way, go the other way. Let go of resistance, we are like currents in the river of life. Resistance will not help us reach our destination. Going with the flow will lead us to many paths.

When it comes down to what is missing, the reason we are not letting go of our old ways of thinking is because we are not giving ourselves permission to shine. We are here to shine our light, to be magnificent in our own unique ways. We are here to support, collaborate and be at one with each other. There is no competition but truly sharing our gifts, blessings and abundance with everyone. When we have this perception, we gain wisdom about why we are here. We become free of attachments and entanglements. We become courageous and bold in our creative expression. We allow ourselves to shine and know that when we shine, we are living our destiny. We are destined to be great and bright like the stars in the sky. Shine your brightest light so others can remember their brightness!

Listening and Opening Your Heart to What Is

Life sometimes becomes too busy with mundane things. We may forget to be still and ask, **"What is important to me right now?"** When we ask this question, we open our hearts to what is in the present. Watching a patient dying today, by her side was her son, who lovingly kissed her on her last breath. This takes me away and brings me to the most vulnerable part of my existence. I called my sons and asked them to have dinner with me, just because I miss them. I shared with them the story of my patient and my son talked about his own experience. He opened up to me that he had been meditating and in his meditation he was picturing me and he was inhaling the painful experiences that I had. He felt pained and heavy, how hard my life had been. He exhaled and sent love and empathy towards me in the spirit. When he shared this to me, I felt my tears running down my cheeks. I felt loved.

These are the special times that we need to build more as we go through our lifetimes. This opens our hearts and allows more love and light to fill our emptiness. We can do this, reach out to your loved ones and be vulnerable. Do not hold back, let go of resentments and procrastination. The time is here, call them and express how you feel and listen to their voices. We are transient beings. The moments that we are thinking of achieving are not here. They are fleeting thoughts of the future. But where is the future? It lies in the present moment.

The actions that we do now, predicts our outcome. When we open our hearts and reach out to others, we build a bridge for deeply meaningful relationships. We burn the old stuff that we no longer need. This is the time to wake up. Let us untie all these knots that we created along the way. Let us see beyond the pain and conflict. Let us strengthen our willpower to reach out and open our hearts to accept others with unconditional love. Listen and open your heart to what is.

When change occurs, we become unsettled to the new realities. We get caught in the mundane and become attached to our comfort zone. We have difficulty letting go and releasing our old ways. Our realities shatter and ask us to take the path of uncertainty. We may go into fear mode and become anxious about the future outcome or afraid of the present moment. We may become restless, not sure of where we are or what will happen in the future. These are the things that we catch ourselves doing or feeling when our realities are shaken or comfort zone tightens. We are used to our roles as a mother or father, or any kind of role that we attach ourselves to. But suddenly, these roles may be taken away and we become unsteady and unstable with our thoughts and emotions.

The first thing to remember is to breathe. Be in your body. Be present. Ask questions that will bring you back to your center. Where are my feelings coming from? Are they healthy for me? Are they loving or coming from fear? What can I do to calm myself and balance the way I think of these changes? Why am I afraid of changes? Will I be taken care of? As you go deeper into asking questions, you will find yourself feeling lighter and calmer.

The anxious thoughts are being revealed. We can see where they are coming from. Like the clouds in the sky, they move and beyond these clouds is a deep clear blue sky. This is our mind. We have a lot of thoughts that cloud our nature, our clear mind. In the expansive and open mind, we have limitless potential and unimaginable possibilities. By being open to all possibilities, we are able to let go freely, with open arms, mind and heart to what the universe is giving us.

This is the path of uncertainty. We are all uncertain of our lives here on earth. No one knows our ending in this physical plane so why put your attention to things that you have no control over. Focus on your blessings and the gifts that this new door offers you.

Think positive and uplift your spirit. You are always provided for. We are just like blades of grass. We are children of the universe. We have limitless potential, especially when we are open to receiving and totally surrendering to our calling.

Our passion will lead us to this path of service. Open and listen to what the universe is giving you. When a door closes, a new door opens. Be here in the present moment and live fully with the knowing that everything is uncertain. Why have these fixations and anxieties about the future when nobody knows what will happen next? Our expectation of our future delays us in building success right before our eyes.

Hone your skills and gifts. Be diligent and your perseverance will bear fruits. Be patient and discipline yourself to be the master of your destiny. You are the co-creator of your life. Design your life to what you want it to look like. You can create magnificently with the knowing that this is your universe. You are blessed to be here, use your mastery and live happily with your creations. Let go of the past, start living here in the now while building your dreams to come true. You are the dream. Dream big!

Clarity on Your Passion

Being clear about your passion creates focus in your daily life. How can you find this clarity? First, we have to know who we are and what makes us happy. There are a lot of qualities within ourselves that we want to bring about but if we do not know what we want, we are lost and scattered in our thoughts. The secret to creating the life you want is knowing yourself and how you can implement your intentions in this reality. Creativity is freedom. Express yourself.

Ask questions about yourself, what do I truly want? List your heart's desires, things that make you happy, what you yearned for as a child. Bring back your childhood, daydream about what you loved to do! This connects you to your emotional body and subconscious mind. These are elements of the driving force to create what we love to do. When we remember these, they trigger us in our core being and reactivate this drive to be successful. Decide who you are. What are the things that you will focus on to create in this life?

For me it is writing, so from now on I declare to the universe that I will be writing every day because this is what I want and it makes me happy to share my thoughts and wisdom. My intention will create what I want. So intention is also a part of being clear and having consistent action towards your goal.

When you do something, do it with excellence. Do not let others opinions affect you. This is your life and you are the captain of your ship. Go with the flow, there are days that are rough but you can always stir into another direction when it does not work. Life is a risk. Take more risks to find your niche. Do not settle for mediocre. Be the highest version of yourself. There is only one you. Be who you are. Be authentic and people will love you for that.

What makes you different from others? These are attributes of yourself that you already know. Look within and reflect on these gifts and journal each day. This helps you create a laser focused destination map of your life. When you know yourself, you will be clear on what you want and execute this consistently. If you missed a day, catch yourself and start all over again. There are no mistakes but only practice will make your work shine as perfect as you want it to be.

Be easy on yourself but be vigilant about your actions. Together with your intentions to do great things, your actions will determine how far you can go with your dreams. Do not give up. The universe brought you here to shine and be a bright star for others. Together we can shine each other's light. Support and collaborate with each other, but first have clarity about your passion so you can attract the right people in your energy fields.

Mastery Of Our Souls

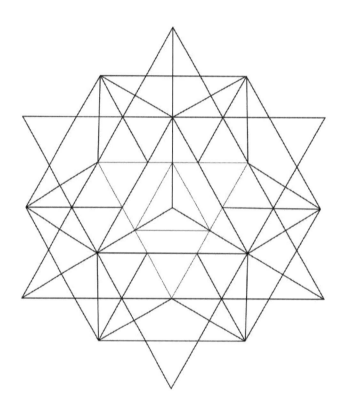

The Ego's Identity

When we are born, we create the ego to grasp this physical dimension because we came from a multi-dimensional space and consciousness. We open our eyes as newly born babies and see this physical reality that we are not aware of. Feeling like an alien, everything is foreign and it puts us in a state of uncertainty. The darkness and gestational stage in our mother's womb is our comfort zone, suddenly we see the light and physical form.

Can you imagine yourself being lost in this physical reality for the first time your eyes open? What do you see? This experience opens the inner eye of the infant and develops emotions and mental thoughts that are attached to the caregivers. As we gather information, we develop false identification from each other's feedback. It molds our core beliefs, conditioning and patterns that become the foundation of our survival mode of existence.

This is the ego's identity. We are not only dealing with this reality but also having to experience our past lives, present and future realities simultaneously in all parallel universes. Our ego has to grasp and attach in order to survive. We are operating from fear when we are in the ego. We forget that we are powerful beings of Light. We get lost in the material world believing this is the only reality that we have. We develop science to prove that creations and God can be investigated and formulated using our methodical minds to prove our thesis.

It is quite exhausting because we keep coming back to our ego. The Ego is never satisfied; it is insecure, fearful, grabs and attaches to what is seen and sensed. Until we reach exhaustion from the endless search for knowledge and return to our heart space, we will not find inner peace. We can fully comprehend that our existence is beyond our ego's point of view. We have to learn to embrace our ego and remain in a vast, open, heart space. We may then be able to integrate our multi-dimensional aspects of being and our ego may find inner peace.

Freedom from Illusions

To master your soul's destiny, you need to be aware of your illusions. This is an important step in being authentic to your true Self, your true essence. We are so bombarded with consumerism, competition and egotistic voices in our heads that it is not easy to listen to the subtle cues of spirit. Spirit speaks softly in our being, touches our heart and makes our soul feel wholesome and loved.

In the world of duality, we are blinded by what we see in front of us and by our attachments to the world. The unseen is where the spirit lives. We have to literally become aware and awaken to our multi- dimensional self to be in a heightened awareness of our evolved consciousness. We cannot change what we see if we keep looking at the external realities of our lives. The manifestation of what we truly want to have in this lifetime will unfold, when we know the truth that lies within and how we can be free of our own illusions.

What are the steps that we can take to be free sentient beings of light?

We have to first know how our ego works and how it presents something that is not real and illusory to our own spirit. With that said, I will lead you to the truth of my experiences as a spiritual healer.

In my younger days, I believed that we are one with all creation. As a child, I was communicating with animals and nature. This is actually the portal for our spirit to connect to the elemental chemistry of our existence as human beings. Because we are incarnated here on our beautiful planet Earth, we need to understand that we are all connected in our existence in this realm. Our mother earth is the portal of this creation and when we want to manifest, we have to be grounded with her magnetic fields to create what our heart desires. The universal and cosmic portal is where we connect and receive the universal light, information and energy that is now available to us. Our evolved human species is now experiencing this ascension because we are in this amazing transformation of our DNA. We are creating and increasing the light molecules in our genes to shift our human consciousness into a Divine nature. It is like heaven on Earth, the paradise and genesis of our light frequency is emitting the luminescence Light of our true being.

Our angelic nature is being revealed to us through Sacred Geometry, numbers and messages. The voices of the angels are being opened to those who can hear and feel these angelic beings of Light. When we are awake, we know these angels around us. We feel, see and hear their messages. But the veil needs to be lifted to reveal their strong presence in our realities. They come to you when you ask them. So ask and you shall receive!

When we are born, we forget where we came from because it would be quite a boring and tedious journey if we knew it all. To be Masters of Light, we need to experience the path of the True Light Divine Ascended Masters. We wanted to experience dichotomy, polarity, vibrations, manifestations, compensations, karma, and all the other universal laws that affect us in our existence right here right now. To master all these energies and vibrations, we have to experience what is light and what is shadow. We had to be clear about what fear is and what love is. This is all part of being human; we are now transcending this vibration and becoming a Divine Conscious Light and Love Being. This is the path of ascension within this human body. Our Light or Soul vibrates into a higher frequency connecting to the universal energy, to The Divine Mind of the Creator or Source of all that is. We radiate this Divine Light to others and they become aware of their own beauty and radiance because of this illuminating pure Light essence that we give out.

Our hearts become an expansive and sacred space like the universe. We understand the codes of God and the creations. We realize that we are all like the stars in the universe radiating this Light to others who are in the dark. We are freed from the illusions of the mind and gain clarity of what our true destiny is. We become empowered, clear and balanced in our walk through life. We become the pure aroma of love. People who come close to our energetic fields feel this truth and vibration. Because of this, we also become aware of our own energetic fields and how we can protect our own auras.

It is imperative to understand why we need protection. We are vibrating at such a high frequency of Light that people who are still asleep will tend to drain or suck our energy unconsciously. So be aware of how energy and light works in this dimension. Our goal is to be a pure Light without draining our own system. We are vessels of this powerful Sacred Light, we need to protect and honor this presence in our existence to be able to serve with full hearts.

The illusions will gradually perish as we master our own true Light and Soul's destiny. We connect fully to the Divine Source of all that is. We become empowered, protected and supported by the magnificent force of God or Source. We know deep in the core of our being what is important, what our goal is, role and mission in this incarnation. We become messengers of Light and love. Together with other awakened Masters of Light, we will create rippling sparks of Light from the Creator and into our Divine and Sacred manifestations. Let us be one with all that is. Shadows, our illusions, are the catalysts to be Masters of our soul's destinies. There is no time and no space in this Divine illumination. Receive this information with open heart and mind. As we free ourselves from illusions, we become Masters of Light.

What is freedom?

Freedom is a state where your spirit is free from distractions of the mundane and liberated from any unconscious state of craving. What are the shadows of freedom? Take an inventory of yourself. Where are you not free to be yourself? What are the things that you are attached to? What blocks your freedom? We are complicated human beings, we get lost in the mundane things of life. We forget to focus. We get lost in the voices in our head or others who are around us. We give our power away. We become mediocre, drained, and powerless. Our creations are vague and have no direction. This is the time to wake up, feel and see; what are your core values? What do you really want?

Today, I am making an inventory of what I truly want. We live our busy lives, lost in the mundane. I feel that our core values anchor us back to what we truly want to create. For me, freedom is a huge component of my life. What is freedom? It is the detachment from anything that is not necessary or that makes me unhappy. I had to learn that attachment to things, people and places, binds me. They block me from being what I want, to be free. I want to be free of all thoughts that do not serve my highest good, including emotions that are low in vibration. Being in alignment with my truth and freedom makes me happy. I am what I am. I am free from clutter, cravings and illusions. I am happy where I am, in a space of freedom and clarity.

The shadows from being free are attachments, clinging to what is not here. That can be the future or worries that we create in our illusions. We only have to be in the present moment. We can be free of all the unconscious thoughts that we create in our mind. Being free from these voices liberates us in our walks of life.

Take an inventory of your life. Ask questions that will help you find your core values. They are the values that are important to you personally. Know yourself. Love and honor these values. They are your guideposts to how you want to live your life. Free your Self from distractions, attachments, and confusions. They create filters and boundaries around you. The things that are important to you make sense in the end. This is your life. No one is living this but you. Be clear. Find inner peace and stillness. Be at peace with your decisions and your core values will direct you to your true essence.

Steps to Spiritual Freedom

In these times of our lives, we have a lot of attachments to things, people and places. We are naturally inclined to bond with these to make us feel loved or safe. This is a part of our human survival instinct. To be detached is not about not loving or caring for others. Rather, it is about being free of any bondage or entanglements from our external world. To be a master of freedom is to be free of attachments and there are a lot of questions in our mind when we want to explore this expansion of our perception.

Freedom is being attuned to our free spirit or soul. As human beings, we need to go beyond this third dimension and be outside of this physical reality. There is an expansive universe within us when we tune into the frequencies of this magnificent light that lies within our chemical structures.

Matter is created from this matrix of energy. However, our souls are eternal. When we are searching for answers, we get lost in the quantum soup of our illusions. The ego has its tricky ways of not being satisfied or fulfilled with what answers we can find to satisfy our thirst of knowledge. We go on like nothing can fill us up. Freedom is being aware of this longing and reaching a point of knowing that everything is given and within our own universe. The answers are all encoded within us, but we are too busy looking outside of ourselves. How did we end up like this, hungry and thirsty, insatiable human beings?

Have you thought of being free? How does it feel to be free? Freedom unloads us of concern of the expectations of others, from the burden that we put on ourselves, from roles that are no longer serving our highest good, from perfection, from being a victim, from sabotaging our own destinies and from being vulnerable. We keep distances from others to prevent feeling hurt. Thus we unconsciously create walls of separation. Fear breeds attachments and when we let go of these attachments, we allow some sense into our creations. We begin to wake up and allow ourselves to be free from these distractions of the ego.

How do we know that we are not free?

When we are caught up with mundane jobs that we are not passionate about, when we settle for less, when we allow people to use us, sabotaging our own selves, when we have no voice in our relationships and when we are attached to others expectations and opinions about us. We have the power to be free. It takes an awakening of our egotistic mind to open and be freed of attachments and illusions. We have this monkey mind that likes to think in the past and future, unconsciously wasting time and space in the present moment that we have right here right now. We need to open our hearts and allow self-love to bloom. Without this we are stuck. We remain small. Yet, we are bigger than what we think we are. We are truly expansive sentient beings of love and light.

Steps to Spiritual Freedom:

1. Know your blockages. We have to understand what our hindrances towards freedom are. By identifying them we can move forward.

2. Release fear and immerse yourself in love. Fear is constrictive. We are going to expand once we let go of fear.

3. Turn your blockages into empowerment. Name the fear and turn it around. For instance, inability to trust can be nurtured gently into trusting our intuition and others.

4. Meditate; find some sacred space for your stillness. Your mind may be too busy and preoccupied to be free.

5. Clean the clutter in your house. A clean house is a clean mind.

6. Let go of things that you are not using. Allow space in your environment.

7. Release guilt and pressure from your vocabulary. They are constrictive and heavy.

8. Other people's opinions of you are not important, focus on yourself.

9. Become aware of your inner critic. Let go of these negative thoughts.

10. Be free from things that are not serving you. Filter your thoughts, words, emotions and actions. Bring light to transcend the victim consciousness.

11. Freedom from ego allows unconditional love to unfold for yourself and others. Be free of negativity. Surround yourself with positive vibrations and people that nurture your soul's growth. Allow this new template of freedom in your existence. The truth will set you free. Be truthful with yourself. Be free!

The Seekers Path

In our soul's journey, we find unanswered questions during our victim consciousness stage. When bad things happen to us, we ask "why me? What is the meaning of life? Who am I? What is my soul's purpose?" Our soul thirsts for the answers to unending questions. We are looking for truth beyond what we are feeling and seeing. Our experiences become more complicated. We become dense, our hearts close and the mind gets busy with thousands of negative thoughts about ourselves and others. We are lost in the dark.

The shadows are the catalysts that open the door for the Light to come in. Embrace this shadow in whatever form it may present itself, totally surrendering to it. Feel and open the doors of your heart, allowing this illuminating light to penetrate your cellular level of memories and consciousness. Ask the Masters of Light to activate your Soul's wisdom that lies dormant inside your heart space. Openly receive the gifts of activations and attunements from the Masters of Light. We are Light Masters. We co-create from this sacred space of Divine love. Our true essence is a spark of Divine's creation in the universe. We are the Universe. Our Soul's destiny is a vast, portal of Light emanating, omniscient, omnipotent and omnipresent Light and Grace from the Source of all creations. It is your passion, the fire that ignites your heart, makes you leap for joy and provides a feeling of oneness. These are your guideposts to what your heart desires.

Find time in stillness, to fully open your heart and mind to God. Listen to the voices in your heart. Allow your emotions to open the floodgates of your heart. Be in awe of your gifts. Be grateful for all your blessings. This is a sacred time and space for your revelation. We can co-create our Soul's destinies with the amazing force and power of God. Live up to your highest good and potential, with gratitude to the Grace of Divine Light. May you find the Light in your search for truth. May God's Divine wisdom be your guide in your Soul's journey. May you shine your bright Light to the Universe.

Mastering our soul's path involves purifying all aspects of our being. The multi-dimensions of our existence are the physical, emotional, mental, spiritual, etheric, and astral bodies that we are made of. To be a Master we need to be an alchemist, purifying our thoughts, words, emotions and actions. This Light that resides in us is a spark of the Source of all that is or the Universe. The Light radiates with luminosity that shines for others to remember their home. The purpose of a spiritual Master is to lead others to see their Divine Light. The spiritual Master has to go through the purification process of humanity in order to be a true empathetic spiritual leader.

The Five Qualities of a Spiritual Master:

1. **INTEGRITY**- Integrity is about the alignment of our mind and heart. When we are congruent with all our thoughts, words, emotions and actions, we become connected to the Divine Light that resides in our subtle body. It is very important to have clear and clean Chakra energy centers to maintain a state of purity. Journaling with our Akashic Records or the blueprints of our souls vibrations will

help heal, clear and release our karmic bondages, attachments, fears, blockages, entities and souls that are attached to our energy fields, including unconscious negative beliefs, unresolved and unforgiven relationships, our negative thoughts and patterns from ancient bloodlines and DNA, curses, drains, hooks or many other things that currently, are not serving our highest good.

When we journal, we create a space for healing, vision, introspection, guidance and direction with clarity and focus. Speak from the heart and not from the mind, this will eliminate clutter in your relationships. Feel what you want to say and deliver with gentleness and kindness. Honesty brings us in alignment to our truth. Checking in with our conscience helps us become wiser and maintain our purest intention.

2. **COMPASSION**- Compassion lies deep in the core of the heart of humanity. We are called to serve with compassion. Witnessing others with compassion reminds us of the rawness and vulnerability of our experience as human beings. We are here to see others as ourselves. We are in the same boat even though it seems like others are suffering. In the collective consciousness of our humanity, we are part of the one. Release judgments and criticisms of self and others.

When we find inner peace, self-acceptance and unconditional love for ourselves, we can magnify these qualities in others. Kindness and compassion brings us together, releasing separation.

3. **AUTHENTICITY**- Being who we are, whatever flaws or imperfections that we have as human beings creates greatness in our spirit. Like the fire that scorches our impurities, we accept our shadows and embrace that we have to create a shift, to

become leaders of our generation. We cannot transform what we do not accept. First, we accept that we have shadows. This is the way to becoming authentic about who we are. We forgive ourselves and others, and then commit to becoming the best version of ourselves.

4. **HUMILITY-** Humility is a simple character of a spiritual Master yet it is so profound to be humble. When we humble ourselves, we give honor to the Divine Source of all that is. It is through this energy that we align our ego with our true essence. Humility is a sign of greatness because we know deep in the recesses of our being that we are here because of the omnipotent power of the One. We are simply an abode to channel this Divine Light that resides in us. Being free of attachment to the roles and titles of our ego is true freedom of spirit.

Be simple and enjoy the fruits of life. Love the people that are around you and validate them for who they are. We are all one regardless of the status quo that can mislead us on our spiritual path.

5. **COMMITMENT-** A spiritual Master is committed to their passion and service. They are dedicated to sharing and giving their gifts to humanity. They are power driven to shine their light and empower others in their soul's journeys. They commit their lives in lifting and inspiring others to a better space. They have big visions. They focus, with clear intention and follow their mission. They spend their time, space and energy towards their goals and soul's purpose. They are consistent with their message and free of distractions, fear and illusions.

Seeing Through the Eyes of the Creator

There are two main emotional signatures in our barometer of our vibrations and frequency. They tell us if we are in alignment with our true light. They are **love and fear**. They are like a continuum of spectrum of light and shadows. Fear would be at the end scale of the barometer and love on the higher scale of vibrations in our energy levels. When we are in the energy of love, we are light and happy. Our body vibrates and glows. When we are in fear, we are in the dark, or shadow, we dim our light. We contract and become small.

Our consciousness is like a vessel holding the vibrations of our frequency. We need to be aware of what type of vibrations we are bringing into our lives. We have to be conscious enough to know that we are responsible for everything that happens in our lifetimes. We have the freewill and choices to navigate our consciousness towards the light spectrum of our personal barometer.

What process shifts our consciousness and transforms the shadows that do not serve our highest good? Shifts are not easy things to do, especially when surrounded by chaos and difficult people. Before we can be in this space of being one, we are called to experience separation from self and others. This is detachment. We need to experience that everything in our life is like a movie projection. We are the projectors of this movie that we create through the lenses of our own eyes.

Our mind that creates thoughts comes from the vast universal mind that created us. We are part of this expansive creation. We co-create everything in parallel universes and multiple dimensions. To tap into our multi-dimensional self, we need to experience freedom from our own physical, mental and emotional bodies. How can we see through the eyes of the creator? We have to understand the components of creation. When we find clarity then we can co-create magnificent lives, feel abundant and secure of our existence, have inner peace, true bliss and love.

The Process of Creation

1. **The projector:** Our souls are the projectors with written blueprints in our Akashic Records. We create everything that happens to us based on different timelines, dimensions and realities: from our past lives, vows, contracts, and agreements that we had partaken in our past, to our karma and how we create the cycle of lifetimes, our conscious, unconscious and sub-conscious mind. Our present moments comprise of the timeline that can guide us if we are in alignment with our Higher Self. The future Ascended Master that we are creating, is also here in these Records as we master our lessons and embody our divine blueprints. We have the power to release, clear and delete any files in our Akashic Records that are not in alignment with our higher self. We are now creating new files, data or programs that will activate our highest potential to install in our data bank.

2. Our **thoughts** receive the information that is stored in the data bank of our Akashic Records, consciously and unconsciously through all timelines, dimensions and realities. We are receiving information, knowledge and wisdom as we tap into our Records. That is why it is important to know, understand and heal our Soul's Records and contracts, to have thoughts that are in alignment with our higher self. When we have confusion, unconscious negative beliefs, patterns and conditioning from our ancient lineage, bloodlines and DNA, these scattered thoughts vibrate at low frequencies. They hinder our mental and emotional bodies from creating magnificent things. Awareness of our thoughts, whether positive or negative, is important to recalibrating our vibrations. Taking responsibility, we wisely choose thoughts that will not harm us.

3. Our **emotions** are guideposts to what is happening in our internal terrain. When thoughts pass by, and when we identify with these thoughts, we suddenly feel these in our heart and energetic body. They attune with each other. For example, in anger, when we start thinking negative thoughts about the other person, we suddenly feel a rush of blood in our veins and sometimes we turn red. We feel these emotions around our gut and heart, telling us that we are being wronged. Our boundaries have been trespassed. Where are these emotions coming from? They are a sum of all our experiences, not only in this lifetime but other timelines. We need to pull out the roots of anger before we can feel inner peace. We need to heal and be able to forgive ourselves and others. Forgiveness is about disengaging the self from all cords of attachments and entanglements from situations and people that do not serve our highest good.

4. Our **filters are our eyes. Our souls** see through our mirrors. If our filters are cloudy; like the lenses in our projectors, then we create and project situations in our lifetime that do not vibrate in light and love. Our vibrations will then, run at a lower frequency. From this, drama, conflict, separation and hardships ensue.

How can we tell if our filters are not working? We have difficulties, challenges and we are not happy. Our true nature is being happy and loving. We become contaminated with our illusion of the ego. The stories that we write will be our eye opener to know if we are living our Higher Self. Our eyes are the windows to our souls.

To see through the eyes of God or Creator, we need to have compassion and forgiveness towards ourselves and others. Our humility will take us there. When we understand that whatever is in our current situation, it is our very creation, and we know that the other person that made us angry is a part of us, then we can release this energetic cord that took us to darkness. Find the shadow or fear. Now look at the opposite of this spectrum and go towards the path of light.

Seeing Darkness For What It Is

Seeing the darkness for what it is requires us to see beyond the shadows that darkness presents. It is a space within the absence of light. When we simplify the meaning of the word, we release attachment or judgment. We are going through a lot of darkness right now in our world. We need to be reminded that this is a spiritual test for all of us. How can we overcome this heavy cloud that is upon us? We have to start with having pure eyes and a new perception.

Primarily, darkness is a part of us. Like the complementary yin and yang, we have darkness like a brother to our evolution of consciousness.

Our divine feminine energy, the receptivity in us, will help heal our shadows. We have to acknowledge this shadow. Where is it coming from? Is it within you? Or attached to you? Once we discover what we are dealing with, perhaps anger, greed, jealousy, lust, these emotions of lower frequency vibrations will show us the way to liberation. These particular emotions will be our catalyst for transformation. Face what you have and allow this to melt down by doing a ritual with the Masters of Light. This force field that you are creating with the intention of releasing and clearing these energies, will help you see and be the light.

Steps in Releasing Darkness

1. Light a candle, meditate, and invoke the Ascended Masters, spiritual guides and teams that you work with. Have your intention ready and know what kind of shadows you are dealing with. Do not judge yourself. Do not resist. Just be. Have your journal ready.

2. Open your Akashic Records and invoke, "Lords of the Akashic Records, please open my book of life, my name is _____ state your legal full name. Create a safe and sacred space for my highest good and healing."

3. Start your prayer, "Masters of Light, Benevolent Masters and my spiritual teams and guides, please assist me in releasing my shadows and darkness. These energies namely _____ for example: anger, guilt, depression, lust, sloth, greed, pride, jealousy, desires, attachments, doubt, hate. "

4. "I ask these energies to go back to the Source of love and light, or transmute to the core of Mother Earth, Gaia. As I now release these energies, I ask the Lords of Karma and the Lords of the Akashic Records to please rewrite my soul's evolution and let it be done. I seal this agreement with the power and force field of the sacred geometrical form of a Merkabah. And so it is."

5. Thank the Masters that have worked with you, "Thank you, thank you and thank you for this portal of healing. Lords of Akashic Records and Lords of Karma please close my book of life. And so it is." Remember to close your Akashic Records every time you open it.

6. You have now created a clear and clean flow of energy with your soul's vibrations in the Akashic Records.

7. The universe will test you and give you situations that will show the same pattern of your attachments. Know that you are always guided and protected. As you become stronger in your faith and totally surrender yourself to service, you will find your life more at peace and in bliss.

8. Manifestations of your creative expression will take place as you become lighter and synchronicity will be in your energy fields.

9. Be at peace with the dark. The darkness is here to help us transmute energies that have been upon us for eons of time.

10. We are the spiritual warriors of Light. Be faithful and surrender to your calling.

Clearing Your Space

As above so below, it is said. When you tap into your soul's Records you will find that you are also clearing your physical space. Energetically, you are clearing and releasing the things and attachments from the past including those that do not serve you anymore. We are all interconnected and the physical dimension that surrounds us has a blueprint of its own. When our soul is ascending, physically we feel lighter.

As we let go of attachments, we loosen the grip of the blocks that keep us disempowered. The more conscious we are about our creations, the more we are able to tap into our highest good. The thoughts, words, emotions that we have, and the actions we do unconsciously become more obvious and more tangible. Everything we can know is recorded in our Akashic Records. We become self-aware. Our intentions and our soul's purpose here on Mother Earth become clearer.

Think of your physical space as your mental space, when your surroundings are messy, your head is literally scattered with all ideas and thoughts that are not grounded. In order to focus on your projects, you have to know that there is order and harmony in universal laws which govern your creations. Like music, every note has to be in synchronicity with the next to create a symphony. The orderliness of your environment will keep your thoughts clear and precise. The external speaks of the internal. Whatever is going on inside you is a mirror of your external environment.

Clearing your space is an important factor to help you clear your thoughts. Becoming a minimalist is a way to filter your busy thoughts and focus your intentions. Whatever it is that you want to create will have a pathway in your mental space and environment. Distractions are our escape from fulfilling our missions. Clear your space and feel lighter in your surroundings. The more you practice this, the more you become clear on what you want to create in your world.

COLLECTIVE COSMIC CREATIONS

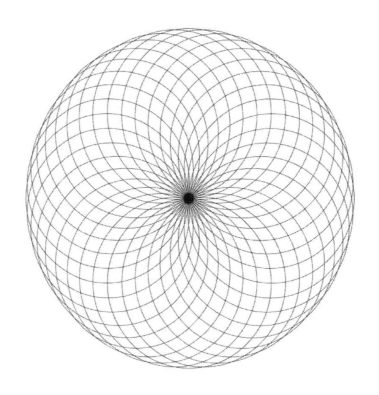

A True Spiritual Master

What is a true master? What does it take to lead from the heart and soul? What are your core values? What is your intention in giving your service? These questions can help you do an inventory of your work as a leader. There are a lot of distractions in our world right now and to be focused, we need to know the roots of our foundation in order to lead in a successful way.

Whatever you are doing, do it from your inner being. Connect with your higher self and allow this to activate your highest function here on earth. We are interconnected in all ways. The difference that makes a master is the fire that burns and ignites the heart to give selflessly. Giving is from a sense of knowing that there is abundance when you believe that we are always provided for.

Steps in mastering your soul's purpose:

1. Be of service from the heart without expectation of receiving.

2. Be bold and courageous. Take challenges as a catalyst to create expansion. Think big!

3. Focus your attention towards your projects. Do not get distracted by others opinions.

4. Know your core values. Why do you do things the way you do? Know yourself.

5. Practice compassion, kindness and gentleness towards yourself and others.

6. Be grateful for all your blessings. Say thank you first thing in the morning.

7. Live in humility. Appreciate everyone for what they do to help you.

8. Celebrate success!

9. Bring joy in the room and be aware of your vibrations.

10. Dance and flow with life. Be aware of resistance. Notice what shows up for you. Take this opportunity and be happy!

Cosmic Creations

What are cosmic creations? They are projects or creations that we intend to do in this physical dimension. They are perceived information and guidance from the cosmic light that is channeled to us. They are bigger than what we think. There is no attachment to the outcome or result to the situation. When we are conscious creators with the divine energy, we are vibrating with a high frequency of love and light.

In our creations, we will encounter universal challenges. What do we do with them? Whenever there is a low frequency of emotion like doubt, or fear, feel this emotion. This is the trigger to knowing that we have a vibration that is not in resonance with our highest good. In the process of clearing, we are purifying our energy fields. Envision the Merkabah in your energy fields and meditate with the Masters of Light.

We are co-creators in this dimension. We have to remember that we are never alone. We are connected to the Masters for assistance, higher guidance, and support. What is in our hands was brought forth by our blueprints. This was written in our Akashic Records. Once we become aware, conscious of our energy fields, we have the power to release and clear them with the assistance of the Masters of Light.

Cosmic creations are beyond our imagination. They come from Divine Intelligence. When they are received with pure intentions coming from a pure heart and soul, they flow with ease and grace. To surrender is one action that will perpetuate this divine flow. We are being called to serve in this way. We are bringers of light for our world. The chaos in our world is a sign of clearing and releasing these energies that no longer serve us. Our neurological pathways are being rewired to create a higher conscious being that is connected to the divine energy at all times. Our Higher Self communicates with our being and it encodes us with the highest good of our incarnation.

Connection with the Source of the divine energy allows access and helps us maintain a high frequency of light and love with all that is and that will ever be. Maintain this space of love and peace. Experience this sacred space. In this space there is openness, light, and expansion. Envision that your house, like your body, is going through a renovation, reinventing yourself. Accept and embrace your shadow side, this is where we learn and are allowed to shine our light brighter. Release all secrets to the light, knowing that you have the birthright in this divine space of creation.

Bathe yourself with ancient wisdom and choose to move forward with a lighted path. Be attuned to your intuition with your inner guidance. You came to transmute any illusion. You are here to remember your divinity, to co-create with your divine blueprint and Source.

The Path of a Conscious Observer

We are blessed to witness the amazing complexities of life. Our "third eye" is being awakened to lift the veils of separation. We are accelerating our frequencies of light and information. The spiritual dimensions are being experienced because of the thinning of the veil. This is now upon us. The sacred geometry of the creations is being revealed to us so we can understand and receive activations within our DNA and subconscious level.

The synergy of all fragments of creation becomes one in harmonious motion. The "I" becomes "We". We are one. The observer is within us and wants to be at one with all that it sees. The seer is one with all creations. There is no separation. When we become the space and the seer, there will be no war or judgments, just one with all that is. This is the space of nirvana: no suffering, all is love.

How do we get to that space of oneness? We have to create a rippling effect of love, light, and peace. By being a conscious observer, we are creating sparks of light that will increase the quotient of light into our Mother Earth. We are the conscious observers. We know how we vibrate and how our thoughts are calibrating in a spectrum of light vibrations.

The higher the frequency, the greater the light and the energy we produce. Our map of consciousness will help us detect our vibrations. The emotions that are vibrating towards love and light are high in this spectrum of consciousness. They bring us situations that are loving and creative.

How to be a conscious observer

1. Do a body scan, how is your state of mind? How do you feel? How is your spirit? What is in your surrounding?

Body-

Mind-

Spirit-

Surrounding-

Be simple and clear, by tuning into your consciousness, you are able to see where you are in the spectrum of light. The heavy, shadows or negative aspects mean that you can transmute them with the Masters of Light. Invoke St. Germaine and the Violet Flame to transmute any energies that are not calibrating in a higher frequency. Call Archangel Michael and the Blue Ray to cut any cords of attachments that are not serving your highest good.

2. Meditate and open your Akashic Records and see where these densities are coming from. Reflect and heal. Bring everything into the frequency of love and light. Feel free from any heaviness. Close the

Records and thank the spiritual Masters that worked with you.

3. Create a daily ritual of meditation and reflection. Walk in nature and ground yourself. Be the conscious observer and witness the beauty of our perfect universe.

Steps to Being a Cosmic Soul

The Cosmic Soul is the universal energy and light coming from the Source of all that is. We are powerful beings of Light. This Light within is connected to the powerhouse of creations, the Akashic fields. Everything that is created in this universe, every thought, word, emotion, intention and action, are here and now, we are in the eternal time and infinite space.

We become a Cosmic Soul when we purify all the densities of our human consciousness such as our toxic mental thoughts and lower emotional vibrations such as anger, worry, anxiety and many other emotions. In this field of oneness with all creation, we become a co-creator of the divine energy flowing within us. As we create, we magnify this love and light beaming within us, radiating the illuminating Light of the Source.

We are beyond our mind. Everything that we think we are is the opposite of what is real. The infinite space is where we want to connect. Creation is from this energy field. When we create from the mind or ego, our work becomes tainted with pride. We have this small self that wants to believe that it is capable of manifesting our desires. It can happen but the root of this creation is built from weaknesses. The true creation is rooted from the spirit of the Source of creation, which is love and light. This is the universal energy, where we tap into an infinite resource of power. Once we understand the purpose of our small self, we are able to integrate our incarnation with greater knowing.

Our emotional fields have to calibrate in the love and light frequency. Any lower vibrations can block us from opening and fully loving our Self and others. The shadows that we are experiencing are here to be released and cleared with the loving assistance of the Masters of Light. Our Cosmic Soul is here; ready to give birth to our new earth. As light workers, we chose this lifetime to anchor this golden Light into our physical dimension. When we are challenged, we are releasing toxins that no longer serve us. This vehicle of Light, which is the Merkabah, will serve as the channel for our multi-dimensional Soul. Activate this with Archangel Metatron and ask him/her to recalibrate our DNA and link us to our divine blueprint and the Akashic Records. The Violet Flame of St. Germaine in the heart of humanity will transmute any energies that are not needed.

We are waves of vibrations in the light spectrum. Recalibrate what does not vibrate in higher frequencies. Creating a ritual with the spiritual guides when you wake up and before you sleep, strengthens your practice of creating a new pattern of DNA.

Steps to being a Cosmic Soul:

1. Create a safe and sacred space. Have this ritual in the morning when you wake up or anytime that is comfortable for you. Meditate and light a candle. Sage or purify your space in the house and yourself. Attune to your spiritual Masters of Light. Open your Akashic Records by invoking the Lords of the Akashic Records to help you open your book of life and state your full legal name that you are using at the current moment. Your name's vibration carries the energies of your Soul.

"Lords of the Akashic Records, please open my book of life and create a safe and sacred space for my highest good and healing. The Records are now open, say this three times."

2. Scan your body, mind, heart, spirit, soul, and other beings in your surroundings. Sometimes you will feel the presence of your loved ones from other dimensions. Journal your way through it, write down anything that comes up. Past life memories can come up.

3. Acknowledge your emotions and mental thoughts, pleasant or neutral. Be aware of what is happening in your consciousness.

4. After scanning, acknowledge and affirm. For example: body -detoxing, mind- clear, heart- heavy, spirit- inspired, soul- goddess like, other beings- angels around me.

5. Be authentic and clear when you are writing down these qualities, do not make it complicated. Do not over analyze. Just tune into your senses.

6. When you feel that there are things that you need to clear, like heaviness around the heart chakra, acknowledge and reflect on the situation that may have caused this condition. Call the Ascended Masters to help you in clearing these energies.

7. Offer forgiveness in your heart chakra for harming others and your Self consciously or unconsciously in all timelines and dimensions.

8. Thank the Masters of Light, the gatekeeper and the Lords of the Akashic Records that worked with you. Close the Records now and say this three times. "The Records are now closed, the Records are now closed and the Records are now closed."

9. Ground yourself after doing this clearing and healing. Eat healthy food, walk in nature, or do some exercise.

10. Give some time for your healing, your body, mind, heart, spirit, and soul are now integrating to become wholesome. Your frequencies and vibrations are calibrating to your Higher Self. Your Cosmic Soul is now attuning into your being. This is a process. Be patient, totally surrendering without attachment to the outcome.

Practice regularly and you will see the transformations within and around you. You will have this new vibrant energy level and happiness. You will see beyond your form. You now have a set of new eyes to see the grandeur beauty of the cosmos for you are one with the universe.

Collective Awakening

As we traverse in our soul's journey, we will find that our paths are all interconnected. We are collectively awakening in our existence. We are never separate. There is no time and space in the present breath that we take. We interlink with the magnanimous creation of the Source of all that is.

With all that said, how can we ascend these shadows that are now so prevalent in our contemporary times? The wars, struggles, sufferings, and confusions that are surrounding us can be a huge distraction from living a clear and clean life. What do we do?

First, we start with our own self. Self-love is the first ingredient for moving beyond pain. This is the micro-mirror of the macrocosm. When we start to understand the true meaning of love, we can truly love others as ourselves. The acceptance and unconditional love that we give ourselves will reverberate in the universe.

Focus your attention on things that bring love, light, peace, and joy. The shadows are always within our egoic mind and we cannot totally let go because we are in our incarnated bodies. When we learn to accept, let go of stories, embrace our shadows, then we can integrate the polar opposites of our spectrum.

Our collective awakening can start happening when we awaken to our own existence. By examining our conscience, beliefs, conditioning, views, ideas, opinions, situations, and relationships, we are able to tune into our truth. We find that it is the opposite of what we think that truly resonates with our hearts wisdom. Finding your triggers will be the catalyst for true transformation. It does not come in one day. It comes as a process. Releasing and clearing all these attachments in our existence will clear our illusions.

The things that are in our fields are awakening us to increase our awareness of what really matters to us. We want our human species to evolve, be safe and feel loved. To ascend our collective consciousness, we have to start with our own Self. As we learn to love and be of service to others, we remember how expansive our souls are. We are one.

About the Author

Teza Zialcita is a powerful spiritual guide who helps you see the bigger picture of your life. She brings clarity and understanding to your conflicts from a soul's perspective, and touches you with her compassionate heart and innate wisdom.

As a wounded healer herself, she helps you find inner peace and resolution with sexual abuse, abortion issues, grieving your child's death, family conflicts, karmic bondages, addictions, and many other blockages that you want to understand, release, clear, and heal.

As a soultrepreneur, she also mentors, guides, and coaches other spiritual healers in creating successful and fulfilling relationships with others and in their own business.

Her fire and passionate drive to create a community that serves holistic healing and health to others, created the Om Healing Community in Vancouver. This spiritual event serves other healers and holds space for our health and consciousness evolution.

Teza's hobbies consist of going out with friends for dinner, dancing, nature walks, and giving crystals to others. Her infectious laughter and positive energy will illuminate your path to healing.

"May I serve you to shine your light brightly in the universe and create a life that is full of love, light, and joy. As we work together, we play with our own inner passion that will guide us to the most exulting and soulful experience of our lifetime!"

Blessings,
Teza

Tezazialcita.com
Akashic-soul-healing.com

More Books by Teza Zialcita

Available on Amazon

IONS OF MANIFESTATION (2017)

UNIVERSAL CONSCIOUS SELF (2013)

Made in the USA
Middletown, DE
21 February 2021